Wonderful Cooking Adventures Await You in the *Woman's Day Collector's Cookbook!*

You'll savor the pleasure of cooking delectable meals, from appetizer to dessert. And if you want to experiment, just follow the clear and concise directions to create different dishes that will satisfy any palate.

There's a complete table of weights and measures to ensure accuracy, and a comprehensive glossary of cooking terms. Tips on everything—from how to make good coffee, to proper storage and freezing of food, to the many uses of kitchen shears—will save you time and ensure success.

Try meals you've never cooked, perhaps never tasted before—and discover the special touches that make familiar menus outstanding—with the

WOMAN'S DAY COLLECTOR'S COOKBOOK

Woman's Day Collector's Cookbook

from the Editors of
__Woman's Day__ Magazine

PUBLISHED BY POCKET BOOKS NEW YORK

POCKET BOOKS, a Simon & Schuster division of
GULF & WESTERN CORPORATION
1230 Avenue of the Americas, New York, N.Y. 10020

ISBN: 0-671-46946-0

First Pocket Books printing April, 1983

10 9 8 7 6 5 4 3 2 1

POCKET and colophon are registered trademarks
of Simon & Schuster.

Printed in the U.S.A.

This is a cook book for connoisseur cooks—a new and unique collection of wonderful food adventures. The recipes it contains have been carefully culled from over 6,500 in the special clip-out sections called Collector's Cook Books that appear each month in *Woman's Day*. The great classics are well represented, and in addition the book offers hundreds of recipes for dishes so unusual that they have seldom or never been published elsewhere. All are organized simply enough for an inexperienced cook to undertake.

Because ingredients, cooking methods and tastes change through the years, every recipe has been brought completely up to date. Final selection was based on testing and tasting by the Woman's Day Kitchen staff and panels of tasters, as well as on the comments sent to us by millions of our readers.

Believing it will make your menu planning easier, your cooking more imaginative and your family's eating more pleasurable than ever, we dedicate the book to all who use and enjoy it.

THE EDITORS

CONTENTS

Woman's Day
Collector's Cookbook

WHAT EVERY GOOD COOK SHOULD KNOW

To Your Success with These Recipes

You will enjoy uniform success with these recipes if you bear in mind the methods, ingredients and measurements with which we developed and tested them.

• All recipes in this book have been tested in the Woman's Day Kitchens with standard American measuring cups (8 fluid ounces = 16 tablespoons), measuring spoons (1 tablespoon = 3 teaspoons) and other standard kitchen equipment.

• Before starting to cook or bake, read the recipe carefully. Assemble all ingredients and equipment, taking care to use the exact pan size specified. Follow recipe exactly. Ingredients are listed in the order of their use. Where directions refer to ingredients by numbers, such as "first 3" or "next 5," a listing with 2 items— "½ teaspoon each cinnamon and nutmeg," for instance —is counted as 1 ingredient.

• Do not increase or decrease recipes unless you are

a skilled enough cook to recognize what adjustments must be made as to ingredients, pan sizes and/or cooking times. Increasing or dividing recipes can be hazardous.

• Preheat oven before baking unless otherwise specified.

• Number of servings given at end of recipe denotes average portions, not number of people the recipe will serve.

• Recipes are not for high altitudes.

• All sugar is granulated white sugar unless otherwise specified.

• Cake flour is sifted before measuring into cup unless otherwise specified. (All-purpose flour need not be sifted before measuring.) To measure either flour, spoon into cup and level off with a straight knife or spatula. No self-rising or unbleached flour is used.

• All baking powder is double-acting.

• All soda is baking soda.

• The exact type of chocolate is specified in each recipe, such as unsweetened squares, semisweet squares, semisweet pieces and sweet cooking chocolate.

• All cornmeal is regular (not waterground) yellow cornmeal unless otherwise specified. No self-rising cornmeal is used.

• All vinegar is cider vinegar unless otherwise specified.

• All brown sugar is firmly packed when measured.

• All confectioners' sugar is sifted before using, unless otherwise specified.

• All commercial syrups are clearly designated as to the type needed for each recipe unless it is not important; i.e., if we do not say dark or light when referring to molasses or corn syrup, either may be used.

• All pepper is ground black pepper unless otherwise specified.

• Fats and shortening are measured at room temperature, packed firmly into measuring cup and leveled off with a straight knife. They should be scraped out of the cup with a rubber spatula.

• Salted butter or margarine, packed in ¼-pound sticks, is used unless otherwise specified. 1 stick = ½ cup = 8 tablespoons = ¼ pound. No whipped butter or whipped cream cheese is used unless specified.

• 1 tall can undiluted evaporated milk (13 fluid ounces) contains 1⅔ cups. Sweetened condensed milk (about 14 ounces) is an entirely different product and *cannot* be used *interchangeably* with evaporated milk. A substitute for buttermilk can be made by putting 1 to 2 tablespoons vinegar in a cup and filling cup with sweet milk. Let stand 5 minutes before using.

• ⅓ to ½ teaspoon dried herbs can be substituted for each tablespoon fresh herbs. Crumble herbs before using, to release flavor.

Cooking Cues

CANDY, JELLY AND FROSTINGS

Use a good candy-jelly-frosting thermometer. One first-rate vertical (non-dial-type) thermometer does all three jobs.

When not in use, hang the thermometer up if possible rather than laying it in a drawer.

Before using each time, test thermometer by boiling in water. If it reads 212°F., cook all recipes to the temperatures given. If it shows a higher or lower temperature reading than 212°F., adjust the temperatures accordingly.

Use a small enough utensil so that the bulb end of the thermometer can be completely submerged in the candy, jelly or frosting, without touching the bottom or side of pot.

Allow plenty of time when making most candies. Many, such as caramels, take long cooking and stirring.

In humid or rainy weather, cook candies 2° higher than the recipe directions.

Use a heavy saucepan, and an asbestos mat, if available, for candies made with milk or cream, since they burn easily.

Watch candy carefully, especially during last few minutes of cooking. Temperature rises quickly at end.

For best results, don't double any of the recipes or make substitutions in ingredients in candies, jellies or frostings

Store different kinds of candies separately. Brittles soften if stored with creamy candies. Airtight storage in a cool place is best for all candies unless otherwise indicated in recipe.

DEEP-FAT FRYING

This means cooking food in enough fat to cover the food completely. When food is properly deep-fried, a thin coating forms on its outer surface, keeping its juices inside and preventing the fat from penetrating into the food.

Properly prepared deep-fried foods are crisp outside, moist and delicate inside. What is more, they have absorbed less fat than foods cooked in a smaller amount of fat. Fat absorption increases with the length of frying time and the size of the surface exposed to the fat. Thus, foods to be deep-fried should either take little time to cook, or should be precooked. Foods should also be cut into small pieces, not more than 2″ to 3″ in diameter, and the pieces should be uniform so that they will cook evenly.

Success with deep-fried foods depends largely on the heat of the fat. It must be hot enough to cause rapid browning of the food's surfaces but the fat should not be so hot that it smokes. The right temperature for most foods is 375°F., although some foods require a higher temperature. Recipes will generally specify the correct temperature when this is so.

Equipment Equipment need not be elaborate. A deep heavy 3- to 4-quart kettle that will hold about 3 pounds of fat is a necessity. There must be enough fat in the kettle to cover the food completely and enough space for the food pieces to move around freely. The kettle should have a flat bottom so that it will sit firmly on the burner, and a short handle to avoid any danger of being overturned. Since the proper temperature is crucial to successful deep-frying, an electric fryer is desirable because the heat is thermostatically controlled.

A wire basket is almost a necessity when deep-frying any quantities of food such as French-fried potatoes. The food is placed in it and then lowered into the fat. The basket makes it easier to get the food in and out and it insures even browning.

A frying thermometer is needed to measure the temperature of the fat. The importance of such a thermometer cannot be sufficiently stressed. While the fat is heating, keep the thermometer in a bowl of hot water to prevent its cracking when it is lowered into the hot fat. Be sure to wipe it very dry before using, because water makes hot fat spatter.

A slotted metal spoon and long-handled metal tongs are also useful for raising and lowering food into the hot fat. And you will need absorbent paper for draining the food.

Fats used in deep-frying should have a high smoking point, i.e., heat to a high temperature before burning. Hydrogenated (solid) fats, lard, and oils such as corn, cottonseed, peanut, olive, sesame and soy are suited for the purpose. Butter and margarine are not; they have low smoking points and burn easily.

After fat has cooled, strain it through several layers of cheesecloth. Use fat again for frying similar foods, such as fat used to fry fish for fish, etc.

When deep-frying frozen foods, remove them from their package, defrost, and thoroughly drain and dry before frying.

Caution Keep a metal lid near the kettle. In case fat should catch fire, drop the lid on the kettle. Fire can also be smothered with salt or baking soda; keep either close at hand. *Never* use water, since this will only spread the flame.

FREEZING

Nearly every type of fresh food can be frozen. Exceptions are: lettuce, celery, cabbage, cucumbers, radishes, cake batters, bananas, custards, cream pie fillings, custard pie, mayonnaise or salad dressing and cooked egg white. Always freeze fresh foods of high quality and at the peak of perfection. Freeze as quickly as possible and don't try to freeze too much food at one time.

Foods must be kept airtight, so select packing materials or containers that are vapor- and moisture-proof. Materials may be made of foil, laminates or polyethylene films. The latter need tape or string. Adjust sizes of packages to fit your family's needs and label and date all foods.

Keep food frozen at 0°F. or lower and do not refreeze if completely thawed. Follow manufacturer's directions for freezing in your particular freezer.

FRUITS AND COCONUT

Buying Fresh Coconuts Fresh coconuts are available year-round but are at their peak during the early winter months. Select coconuts heavy for their size that sound full of liquid when shaken. Avoid those with wet or moldy eyes.

Storing Fresh Coconuts Store unopened coconuts at room temperature. Grated coconut and unused pieces should be kept tightly covered in refrigerator or freezer.

Preparing Fresh Coconuts Pierce eyes in end of coconut and drain off liquid; reserve if needed in individual recipe. Put coconut in shallow pan in moderate oven (350°F.) 20 minutes, or until shell cracks in several places. Remove from oven and pound with hammer or mallet to crack shell open. Remove coconut meat and cut off black outer shell. Coconut pieces can then be eaten like any nut. Or for use in recipes, grate meat on grater or whirl a few small pieces at a time in blender until finely grated or shredded.

Packaged Coconut Sweetened coconut, in cans or bags, comes flaked, grated (cookie coconut) and shredded. Length of shreds and moisture content vary. Frozen unsweetened coconut and coconut syrup, honey and chips are also available. Coconut syrup is made by adding sugar to the emulsion obtained by pressing coconut and cooking it to form a syrup. It is used for milk shakes and as a sauce. Coconut honey is similar but the cooking time is longer and the brown skin on the coconut meat is not removed. The honey is used as a spread.

Coconut chips are thin chips of toasted coconut, salted and used as a snack.

Dried-fruit Tips Most dried fruits available nowadays don't need soaking or long cooking. Occasional exceptions are fruits sold in bulk. To cook these, cover with water and slowly bring to boil. Cover and simmer until tender. Cook apples and apricots 20 to 30 minutes; nectarines and peaches, 45 minutes; pears, 35 minutes; prunes, 45 minutes; raisins, 10 minutes. Pitted prunes are available now and are a great convenience. Follow directions on label for cooking packaged fruits. Sweeten after cooking. (Honey makes a delicious sweetener.)

To snip dates and raisins Oil scissors or rinse in hot water before using.

To plump prunes Put fruit in jar or bowl and cover with cold water, allowing 1 quart water to 1 pound prunes. Cover and soak 24 hours. Refrigerate and use as needed.

To store dried fruits Store fruits tightly covered in cool, dry, well-ventilated place; in hot weather, in refrigerator.

FRUITCAKE TIPS

Preparation Different combinations of fruits and nuts can be used in any fruitcake, but the total amount should be the same as given in the recipe. Chop or slice the fruits and nuts a day or so before making the cake, if more convenient, and refrigerate.

Glazing and Decorating Before serving or gift-wrapping cakes, you can glaze and decorate them. Melted tart jelly or equal parts of honey or corn syrup and water, boiled 2 minutes, can be brushed warm on cold cakes. Press into glaze designs made of candied cherries and nuts; leaves cut from citron angelica or green candied cherries; and slices of red or green candied pineapple. Brush again with glaze and put in slow oven (300°F.) about 10 minutes to set. Glazed dried fruits such as prunes and apricots make attractive decorations. To prepare, cover fruits with water and simmer, covered, 10 minutes; drain. Bring to boil equal parts of honey, sugar and water. Add fruits and simmer about 15 minutes. Drain on cake rack. Remaining mixture can be used to glaze cake. Fruitcakes aren't usually frosted but the top can be spread with almond paste and a thin layer of confectioners'-sugar frosting. For the frosting, mix 1 cup sifted confectioners' sugar, 1 egg white and a few drops of almond extract. Melted semisweet chocolate is a good substitute for the frosting on white fruitcakes.

Serving Fruitcakes, especially dark ones, are better if allowed to age a week or two before eating. Chilled cakes usually cut best. Slice thin with a serrated knife, if available. If not, use a thin sharp knife.

Storage Dark fruitcakes keep better than light ones since the larger proportion of fruit to batter adds moisture. Both types keep better if refrigerated. They can also be frozen. When refrigerated, they should be wrapped in foil, waxed paper or plastic and, if possible, put in airtight container. Dark cakes can be wrapped first with a cloth soaked in brandy, wine or bourbon. Liquor should not be put on white fruitcakes since it may make them soggy. Wrapped and refrigerated, dark cakes will keep several months, light ones about 2 weeks. Dark cakes will, of course, ship better.

GARNISHES

Garnishes are the small decorative touches you add to a plate or platter to make a dish more attractive and to give food color and taste contrast. They may be sweet, spicy or simply crisp and cool. Often they are merely raw fruits or vegetables cut into fanciful shapes. However you use them, just keep these two rules in mind.

• Don't overlook the beauty of the food itself. When carefully selected and well prepared, food is attractive by virtue of its natural goodness and freshness and its varying textures, colors and aromas. Just a row of thinly cut, beautifully roasted meat slices, delicately crusted, covered with a silky shimmer of sauce and garnished with mushroom slices and fresh perky bunches of watercress, is beautiful to look at. Good food, good design involving color, form and pleasing combinations all add up to successful garnishing.

• Be sure the garnishes are in keeping with the food itself, and that the food is arranged on platters or in dishes suitable for it.

GELATIN

Large Molds Attractive molds are available in a variety of shapes and sizes. There are shells, pineapples, fish and many other shapes. However, square cake pans, loaf pans or mixing bowls can also be used. Mixtures can be unmolded and cut in squares or slices, or scooped out with an ice cream scoop.

Individual Molds A selection of scalloped, fluted and other shapes is available. Mixtures can also be molded in custard cups, coffee cups or even paper cups. Some mixtures need not be molded but can be spooned directly into sherbet or parfait glasses before chilling.

Molding Allow at least 3 hours chilling time for gelatin-based mixtures to become firm. Some may need to chill overnight before being turned out of mold. Refrigerators also vary in degree of coldness and this must be considered.

Unmolding Dip mold in warm water to the depth of the gelatin. Loosen around edge with the point of a paring knife. Put serving dish on top of mold and turn upside down. Shake, holding the dish tightly to mold.

Using Fruit Juice or Syrup Fresh or frozen pineapple juice and fruit must be boiled 2 minutes before being added to gelatin mixtures. Fresh pineapple contains an enzyme that destroys the gelling power of the gelatin. Use not more than ½ to ¾ cup canned-fruit syrup in a recipe calling for a total of 2 cups liquid. These syrups may be too heavy and sweet and prevent the mixture from gelling properly.

GIFTS OF FOOD

Containers A glass or plastic container or a covering of transparent plastic is perfect for many food gifts since they are so attractive and look so appetizing they really need no further decoration. Foil containers, such as loaf pans, trays and fluted cupcake pans, and reusable containers, such as apothecary jars, baskets, brandy snifters, trays, painted wood or metal boxes and miniature bread trays, can also be used. Frozen-pudding containers and coffee cans with snap-on lids are also fine; the pudding containers have attractive colored lids. Plastic drinking glasses can be used for some foods. Cotton rug yarn comes in many colors and is convenient and is inexpensive for tying gifts.

Decorating Jar Lids Jelly or pickle jars make attractive containers. To decorate the lids, cover with foil, felt or crepe paper; or attach bows, artificial fruits or flowers, or a small ornament with double-faced masking tape.

Decorating Glass Containers Use notary seals (they come in several sizes and colors), make stripes with colored plastic tape, cut designs out of self-adhesive plastic, or make appropriate holiday drawings with china markers.

To Trim Jar Lids with Yarn or Cord With toothpick, thinly spread screw-type jar lids with white glue. Starting at edge of rim, carefully wind red or green yarn or cord around lid, keeping rows very close together. (Guiding yarn or cord with toothpick prevents it from sticking to fingers.) Reapply small amounts of glue, if necessary. At center, cut yarn or cord, leaving about ½" length. Apply small amount of glue to end and tuck under, using a clean toothpick. Let stand until glue is dry.

When to Make Sealed gifts: anytime. Refrigerated gifts: no more than a day or two before giving. Cakes: unless frozen, no more than a week ahead. Candies: no more than a week ahead. Breads: unless frozen, no more than two days ahead. Label food gifts that require refrigeration. Serving suggestions are helpful, too.

Cookies for Mailing Select ones that keep their fresh flavor at least a week under average conditions. Those low in eggs are best. Choose thick, firm cookies that won't break easily and end up in crumbs.

Wrapping for Mailing Wrap separately in transparent plastic wrap or foil. Pack in crumpled tissue paper in a firm box so cookies cannot slide around. Gift-wrap, then cover with corrugated cardboard. Put in a slightly larger box and mark it "Fragile." *Important* Food gifts that require refrigeration should be so labeled, and those that require reheating should carry a decorative tag or label with the reheating directions. Serving suggestions might prove helpful, too.

Something Extra Include the recipe for your gift either

typed or neatly handwritten on a small card that the recipient can transfer to her recipe file for future use. Sign your name and add the date.

GRATING AND SHREDDING

These are not the same and should not be confused.

To grate is to reduce a hard food into smaller pieces by rubbing against a rough or indented surface. Spices, hard cheeses, lemon or orange peel, onions, cabbage and potatoes are grated to bring out their flavor and to make them easier to mix with other food. There are hand graters, wire graters and mechanical graters in different shapes so they may be placed over a bowl or loaf pan, or stand on the table for grating.

To shred is to tear or cut into fragments or strips. It may be done with a sharp knife by cutting on a board or on a mechanical or hand shredder. Some hand and mechanical shredders also have disks or sides with different-size cuts for making small, medium or large cuts.

HONEY

Measuring Honey When baking with honey, measure the shortening first and then measure the honey in the same cup. The honey will slide out more easily.

Storing Honey Store honey in a dry place, because it absorbs and retains moisture. Do not refrigerate. Refrigeration or freezing won't harm the color or flavor, but it may hasten granulation. If granulation, or solidification, does occur, put the container in a bowl of warm water (no warmer than the hand can bear), until the crystals melt and the honey liquefies.

Kinds of Honey Five types of honey are on the market

today: liquid (used in our recipes); granulated, or solid, sometimes called candied, creamed or honey spread; comb; cut comb, which comes in bars about 4" long and 1½" wide; and chunk, which is small pieces of comb honey in liquid honey.

Buying Honey Buy the flavor of honey you prefer, either very mild or strong. The flavor depends on the flower from which the bees gather nectar. As a rule, the lighter the color of the honey, the milder the flavor. Mild-flavored clover honey should be used in baking. The moisture content varies in the less common types of honey, such as tupelo, sage, orange-blossom, buckwheat and many others, and this may unbalance the recipe. Serve these stronger types as spreads in order to appreciate more fully their unusual flavors.

KNIVES

Cut working time by having good-quality and sharp knives. Do not let these precious tools of your trade be misused by anyone. Use the type of sharpener recommended by the manufacturer. Buy knives to fit your hand and purpose. If you have not mastered the art of using French knives and a good solid wooden chopping board or block, learn how. Properly used, a French knife requires a minimum of time, energy and clean-up to chop or mince almost any food.

LUNCH BOXES

Soups

• Freeze individual cans of flavored bouillon (or fruit or vegetable juice) and pack them frozen. At lunchtime they'll be the right temperature for drinking. Use miniature can openers for these.

• Tie a string around a frankfurter and dangle frankfurter in thermos of hot tomato juice, tomato soup, pea or bean soup. At lunchtime, remove heated frankfurter and put in split roll. Drink liquid.

• Put soups in wide-mouthed vacuum containers and include a sturdy plastic ladle spoon.

Sandwiches and Such

• For non-soggy sandwiches, spread softened butter or margarine evenly to the edge of each bread slice. Peanut butter and moistened cream cheese also keep moist fillings from soaking into the bread.

• For easier eating, use several thin slices of meat rather than a single thick one.

• Wrap lettuce, tomato slices, pickle slices and other juicy items separately in moisture-proof wrapping to be added to sandwich later.

• Tuck in small salt and pepper shakers and little packets of catsup, jelly, mustard and mustard relish, whichever are appropriate. Tiny plastic containers with covers can also be used for mustard, etc.

Tips on Freezing Prepare a week's supply of sandwiches, wrap individually and freeze. Pack in lunch boxes while still frozen and they'll be just thawed by lunchtime. Don't keep frozen longer than 2 to 3 weeks. All fresh breads freeze well. For fillings, use cooked egg yolk, peanut butter, cooked chicken, turkey, meat, fish, dried beef or drained crushed pineapple. Do not use very moist fillings, cooked egg white or raw vegetables. For binders use lemon, orange, pineapple or other fruit juice; milk; dairy sour cream or applesauce. Avoid

mayonnaise or salad dressing, which separate when they
are frozen. Good combinations are: minced hard-
cooked egg yolk with sour cream and chopped dill
pickle, grated cheese with sour cream and chili sauce,
thinly sliced ham with cream cheese and chopped
chives, chopped chicken with sour cream and red-pep-
per relish, and liver pâté with crumbled crisp bacon.

Quickies

• Alternate cheese and ham cubes on small skewers
or picks. Wrap with bread-butter sandwiches.
• Hollow out frankfurter or sandwich rolls and fill
with tuna or chicken salad.

MERINGUES

A meringue is a mixture of beaten egg whites and
granulated sugar. It may be soft or hard depending on
the amount of sugar added during the beating. Soft
meringue may be used as a topping for pies, cakes and
puddings; hard meringue as a pastry shell for fruit or
ice cream. Here, rules for perfect meringues:
• Separate eggs while they are cold.
• Allow egg whites to warm to room temperature,
since at this temperature they can be beaten to incorporate more air.
• Use a small deep bowl and a beater free from
grease, as fat interferes with the proper beating of egg
whites. The whites will increase to 2½ to 4 times their
original volume. A rotary hand beater can be used in
making a soft meringue; an electric mixer is necessary
for a hard meringue.

• When egg whites have been beaten to the foamy stage, add salt and cream of tartar (1 teaspoon to one cup unbeaten egg whites).

• The addition of sugar determines the type of meringue produced. Two tablespoons granulated sugar per egg white results in soft meringue. Four to 5 tablespoons of sugar for each egg white are added for hard meringues. Beat in sugar gradually, 1 tablespoon at a time, until no grains of sugar can be felt when a little is rubbed between the fingers. Meringue should form pointed peaks that are so stiff they stand upright and don't curl over.

• When spreading a meringue on a pie or cake, be sure to spread it over the entire surface, so the filling is completely covered and the meringue is attached to the edge of the dish. This prevents shrinkage of the meringue during baking.

• When preparing a hard meringue, spoon or pipe it onto unglazed brown paper for easier removal when done.

• To prevent "weeping" in a soft meringue, bake it in a preheated moderate oven (350°F.) for 12 to 15 minutes, or until golden brown. Cool at room temperature and it will not bead. Bake an individual hard meringue (tart size) in a preheated very slow oven (275°F.) for 45 minutes, then reduce heat to 250°F. and bake another 15 minutes until very lightly golden and hard to the touch. Bake larger hard meringues (pie size) in a preheated very slow oven (275°F.) for 1 hour. The oven temperature should always be low to dry the meringues and make them crisp instead of gummy.

• A meringue mixture can also be poached in milk and used to top a soft custard.

• Allow hard meringues to cool in the oven.

OVEN-TEMPERATURE CONTROL

In baking, exact temperature control is extremely important for some foods—namely cakes, pies, breads, soufflés, popovers, cream puffs, meringues and custards. In others, a little variation can be tolerated; for example, some casserole dishes, baked potatoes, beans, meat loaves, etc. However, it is always desirable to have oven temperatures as accurate as possible. And since temperatures may vary for any one of a number of reasons, we suggest the following checks.

• When a range has no thermostatic oven control, a portable oven thermometer can be a great help. Check the temperature frequently and adjust the amount of heat manually.

• Use a portable oven thermometer to determine the accuracy of an automatic thermostatic control. If, for example, your oven is set at 375°F. but the thermometer shows 350°F., turn the control up an extra 25° to compensate.

• Some thermostatic controls are accurate in the middle temperature range but inaccurate at very high or very low temperatures. So whenever you're baking one of the dishes listed above it's a good idea to check your oven out.

SHEARS

Good sharp kitchen shears are most useful in the kitchen. It pays to buy a good quality of stainless steel; the type that separates into 2 parts for cleaning is most convenient. These may be sharpened easily, and washed in the dishwasher (non-stainless shears rust in the dishwasher). Here are a few tips for putting shears to work for you.

1. Snip small amounts of parsley, green onion, celery, watercress, capers, pimiento, etc.
2. Use in boning fish or poultry.
3. Cut off bread crust if doing only one or two slices.
4. Snip raw or cooked bacon into small pieces for recipe use.
5. Disjoint poultry.
6. Open frozen food package wrappings.
7. Snip cord for trussing poultry, tying meat rolls, etc.
8. Cut up dried fruits.
9. Cut marshmallows and dates (wet first).
10. Cut out membranes from liver, kidneys, etc.
11. Trim fat off chops, cutlets, steaks, etc.
12. Cut cross in baked potato skin before serving.
13. Cut around sections and remove center from grapefruit halves.

Tables of Measures and Weights

LIQUID MEASURE

1 dash	= 6 drops
1 teaspoon	= 1/3 tablespoon
1 tablespoon	= 3 teaspoons
1 tablespoon	= 1/2 fluid ounce
1 fluid ounce	= 2 tablespoons
1 jigger	= 3 tablespoons
1 jigger	= 1 1/2 fluid ounces
1 gill	= 1/2 cup
1 cup	= 1/2 pint

1 cup	= 16 tablespoons
1 cup	= 8 fluid ounces
1 pint	= 2 cups
1 pint	= 16 fluid ounces
1 fifth	= 25 fluid ounces
1 quart	= 2 pints
1 quart	= 4 cups
1 quart	= 32 fluid ounces
1 gallon	= 4 quarts
1 gallon	= 16 cups
1 gallon	= 128 fluid ounces

DRY MEASURE

1 dash	= less than ⅛ teaspoon
1 teaspoon	= ⅓ tablespoon
1 tablespoon	= 3 teaspoons
¼ cup	= 4 tablespoons
⅓ cup	= 5 tablespoons plus 1 teaspoon
½ cup	= 8 tablespoons
⅔ cup	= 10 tablespoons plus 2 teaspoons
¾ cup	= 12 tablespoons
⅞ cup	= 14 tablespoons
1 cup	= 16 tablespoons
1 pint	= 2 cups
1 quart	= 4 cups
1 peck	= 8 quarts
1 bushel	= 4 pecks

AVOIRDUPOIS WEIGHT

1 ounce	= 28 grams
¼ pound	= 4 ounces
½ pound	= 8 ounces
1 pound	= 16 ounces

OVEN TEMPERATURES

Very slow oven	250°—275° F.
Slow oven	300°—325° F.
Moderate oven	350°—375° F.
Hot oven	400°—425° F.
Very hot oven	450°—475° F.
Extremely hot oven	500°—525° F.

Internal Temperatures for
DONENESS IN MEAT AND POULTRY

Beef, rare	140° F.
medium	160° F.
well done	170° F.
Lamb	175°—180° F.
Pork (loin)	170° F.
Pork (other cuts)	185° F.
Veal	170° F.
Ham (uncooked)	160°—170° F.
Ham (fully cooked)	130° F.
Turkey (whole)	180°—185° F.
Chicken	185° F.
Capon and Duckling	190° F.

Temperatures for
DEEP-FAT FRYING

Chicken	350° F.
Doughnuts and fritters	350°—375° F.
Fish and seafood	350°—375° F.
Croquettes	375°—385° F.
Vegetables	375°—385° F.
Potatoes	385°—395° F.

Temperatures for
CANDY, FROSTING AND JELLY-MAKING

Jellying point	220° F.
Thread	230°—234° F.
Soft ball	234°—240° F.
Firm ball	244°—248° F.
Hard ball	250°—266° F.
Soft crack	270°—290° F.
Hard crack	300°—310° F.

GLOSSARY

BAKE To cook in an oven or oven-type appliance. Covered or uncovered containers may be used. When meats are baked in uncovered containers, the method is called roasting.

BAKING SHEET A flat, rectangular utensil closed on all four sides. Used where protection of the sides is necessary to prevent juicy fillings or other mixtures from running off sheet into the oven.

BARBECUE To roast slowly on a grill or spit, over coals or under free flame or oven electric unit, usually basting with a highly seasoned sauce. Popularly applied to foods cooked in or served with barbecue sauce.

BASTE To moisten meat or other foods while cooking to add flavor and to prevent drying of the surface. The liquid is often melted fat, meat drippings, fruit juice or sauce.

BATTER A mixture of flour and liquid, usually combined with other ingredients, as in baked products. The mixture is of such consistency that it may be stirred with a spoon and is thin enough to pour or drop from a spoon.

BEAT To mix rapidly 1 or more ingredients, to make mixture lighter, frothier or smoother, with a brisk, regular motion that lifts the mixture over and over, using a fork, spoon or whisk, or with a rotary motion as with an egg beater or electric mixer.

BLANCH *(precook)* To preheat in boiling water or

steam. (1) Process used to inactivate enzymes and shrink some foods for canning, freezing or drying. Vegetables are blanched in boiling water or steam, and fruits in boiling fruit juice, syrup, water or steam. (2) Process used to aid in removal of skins from nuts, fruits and some vegetables.

BLAND Mild-flavored, not stimulating to the taste.

BLEND To mix thoroughly two or more ingredients.

BOIL To cook in water or a liquid consisting mostly of water in which bubbles rise continually and break on the surface. The boiling temperature of water at sea level is 212°.

BRAISE To cook meat or poultry slowly in a covered utensil in a small amount of liquid or in steam. (Meat may or may not be browned in a small amount of fat before braising.)

BREAD CRUMBS *Soft bread crumbs* are made by crumbling day-old or slightly stale bread. Firm bread is best for these. *Dry bread crumbs* are made from dry, hard bread. Crumbs can be made by whirling broken bread in blender or rolling with rolling pin. *Fine dry bread crumbs* are commercially packaged crumbs. They are sold plain or seasoned and are used for breading, etc.

BREADED Coated with crumbs of bread or other food; or coated with crumbs, then with diluted slightly beaten egg or evaporated milk, and again with crumbs.

BROIL To cook by direct heat.

CAKE PAN Utensil for baking cake. It may be round, square or oblong, with straight or slightly flared sides. Some have removable bottoms and some, a tube in the center. Size is designated by dimensions (to nearest 1/4") of top inside rim.

CANDIED (1) When applied to fruit, fruit peel or ginger, cooked in a heavy syrup until plump and translucent, then drained and dried. The product is also known as crystallized fruit, fruit peel or ginger. (2) When applied to sweet potatoes and carrots, cooked in sugar or syrup.

CARAMELIZE To heat sugar or foods containing sugar until a brown color and characteristic flavor develop.

CASSEROLE A covered utensil in which food may be baked and served. It may have one or two handles. Size is stated in liquid measurements.

CHAFING DISH A utensil used to cook food at the table, consisting of a deep, lidded skillet that sits on a stand over a burner. Some are like a double boiler, with a pan for hot water into which the skillet may be placed.

CHICKEN FRYER A deep, covered frypan or skillet.

CHOPPED Cut in pieces with a knife or other sharp tool.

CLARIFIED BUTTER The upper portion of butter, clear, liquefied and oil-like, formed when butter is melted slowly, then cooled without stirring.

CLARIFY To make a liquid clear and free from solids, such as broth made clear by the use of egg white.

COOKIE SHEET A flat, rectangular utensil that may be open on one, two or three sides. Especially designed for baking cookies and biscuits.

CREAMED (1) One or more foods worked until soft and creamy, using a spoon, wooden paddle or other implement. Applied frequently to mixing or blending fat and sugar together. (2) Applied to foods cooked in or served with a white sauce.

CUSTARD CUPS Small, deep, bowl-shaped utensils for oven use. They contain individual servings.

CUT IN To distribute solid fat in dry ingredients by chopping with knives or pastry blender until finely divided.

DASH Less than 1/8 teaspoon of an ingredient, usually a spice.

DECORATE To embellish a dessert with ingredients that add color or flavor, such as whipped cream or topping, bits of candied fruit, maraschino cherries, etc.

DICE to cut into small cubes.

DOUBLE BOILER Consists of two saucepans (each with a handle or side handles) that fit one on top of the other. Food that must be cooked at a low temperature is placed in top pan over hot or boiling water in the lower pan.

DREDGE To coat or sprinkle food with specified ingredient, such as flour.

DRIPPINGS Fat and juices drawn from meat during cooking.

DRIZZLE To sprinkle in small amounts or particles.

DUTCH OVEN A large heavy pot with a tight-fitting cover, especially good for long, slow cooking.

FOLD To gently combine ingredients for maximum volume and lightness by using two motions, one that cuts vertically through the mixture and another that turns the mixture over as the implement slides across bottom of mixing bowl.

FREEZE-DRYING A process to preserve foods by freezing and drying them in a vacuum. Freeze-dried food is porous, brittle and lightweight. It also retains its original shape when rehydrated, and can be stored without refrigeration.

FREEZING A method of preserving food by chilling it very rapidly at a low temperature (usually —10°F. or below) and maintaining it at a temperature below 0°F. Freezing is accomplished by direct immersion in a refrigerating medium, such as brine; by indirect contact with a refrigerant, such as conduction through metal plates; or by a blast of cold air. In flash freezing, food is frozen at very low temperatures in a medium such as liquid nitrogen.

FRENCH FRYER An uncovered cooking utensil with a perforated, meshed or sieve-like insert basket with one handle, used for deep-fat frying of foods.

FRICASSEE To cook by braising. Usually applied to meat, poultry and game cut into pieces.

FRY To cook in fat. Applied especially to (1) cooking in a small amount of fat, also called sautéing or panfrying; (2) cooking in a deep layer of fat, also called deep-fat frying.

FRYPAN OR SKILLET A shallow covered or uncovered pan with one handle. Size is stated by the top diameter in inches.

GARNISH To embellish a main dish or salad with ingredients that add color or flavor, such as parsley, paprika, radish roses, carrots curls, etc.

GLAZE To coat with a thin sugar syrup cooked to the hard-crack stage (300°F.). When used for pies and certain types of bread, the mixture may contain thickening, but is not cooked to such a concentrated form, or it may be uncooked.

GRIDDLE A very shallow, uncovered, smooth, heavy utensil (occasionally with pouring lip) equipped with one or two handles. Size is stated by top outside dimension.

GRILL To cook by direct heat. Also a utensil or appliance used for such cooking.

GRIND To reduce to particles by cutting or crushing.

KETTLE A covered or uncovered cooking utensil with a bail handle. Capacity is stated in liquid measurement.

KNEAD To manipulate with a pressing motion accompanied by folding and stretching.

LARD To cover with strips of fat, or to insert fat strips into meat with a larding needle.

LOAF PAN A deep, narrow, rectangular utensil with slightly flared sides; designed for oven use.

LUKEWARM Approximately 95°F.; tepid. Lukewarm liquids or foods sprinkled on the wrist will not feel warm.

MARINATE To put food in a marinade, a seasoned or flavored liquid, to give flavor.

MASK To cover completely. Usually applied to the use of mayonnaise or other thick sauce.

MINCE To cut or chop into very small pieces.

MIX To combine ingredients in any way that effects a distribution.

MUFFIN OR CUPCAKE PAN A tray-like utensil consisting of a number of suspended individual cups that are almost straight-sided and that are an integral part of the pan.

OPEN ROASTING AND BAKING PAN A large rectangular pan especially designed for roasting meats and poultry and for baking.

PANBROIL To cook uncovered on a hot surface, usually in a frypan. Fat is poured off as it accumulates.

PANFRY To cook in a small amount of fat. (See FRY and SAUTÉ.)

PARBOIL To boil until partially cooked. Usually cooking is completed by another method.

PARE To cut off the outside covering.

PEEL To strip off the outside covering.

PIEPANS OR PIE PLATES Round, open utensils with flared sides, especially designed for baking pies.

POACH To cook in a hot liquid using precautions to retain shape. The temperature used varies with the food.

POT ROAST A term applied to cooking large cuts of meat by braising or to the meat so cooked. (See BRAISE.)

PRESSURE COOKER An airtight container for cooking food at a high temperature under steam pressure. It is equipped with a gauge for measuring and indicating the pressure on a graduated dial or with some other device. Pressure cookers are used in canning low-acid foods, for cooking less tender cuts of meat and poultry in reduced time and for cooking some vegetables.

RECONSTITUTE To restore concentrated foods to their normal state, usually by adding water. Applied to such foods as dry milk (for fluid milk) or frozen orange juice (for liquid juice).

REHYDRATION To soak, cook or use other procedures with dehydrated foods to restore water lost during drying.

RENDER To free fat from connective tissue at low heat.

ROAST To cook uncovered in hot air. Usually done in an oven, but occasionally in ashes, under coals or on heated stones or metals. The term is usually applied to meats, but may refer to other foods such as potatoes, corn or chestnuts.

ROASTER A covered pan, with or without a rack. Especially designed for cooking meats and poultry. Length and width are measured overall outside the pan, including handles.

ROTISSERIE An appliance designed to roast meat or poultry by dry heat on a turning spit.

SAUCEPAN A covered or uncovered cooking utensil with one handle. Capacity is stated in liquid measurement.

SAUTÉ To brown or cook in a small amount of fat. (See FRY.)

SCALD (1) To heat milk to just below the boiling point, when tiny bubbles form at edge. (2) To dip certain foods in boiling water. (See BLANCH.)

SCALLOP To bake food (usually cut in pieces) with a sauce or other liquid. The food and sauce may be mixed together or arranged in alternate layers in a baking dish, with or without a topping of crumbs.

SEAR To brown the surface of meat by a short exposure to intense heat.

SIMMER To cook in a liquid just below the boiling point, at temperatures of 185°F. to 210°F. Bubbles form slowly and collapse below the surface.

STEAM To cook in steam with or without pressure. The steam may be applied directly to the food, as in a steamer or pressure cooker.

STEAMER A covered saucepan or sauce pot having one or more perforated insert pans equipped with a handle or handles.

STEEP To allow a substance to stand in liquid below the boiling point for the purpose of extracting flavor, color or other qualities.

STERILIZE To destroy microorganisms. For culinary purposes this is most often done at a high temperature with steam, hot air or boiling liquid.

STEW To simmer in a small quantity of liquid.

STIR To mix food materials with a circular motion for the purpose of blending or securing uniform consistency.

TEXTURE Properties of food including roughness, smoothness, graininess, etc., that are visible or sensed with the skin and the muscles in the mouth.

TOAST To brown by means of dry heat.

UTENSILS FOR BAKING AND TOP-OF-RANGE COOKING Inside dimensions (to nearest ¼″) of baking utensils are used to designate size. Most utensils are measured from the top inside for length, width or diameter. In general, capacities are stated in liquid measurements when level-full.

WARM A temperature of 105°F. to 115°F. for liquid or food.

WHIP To beat rapidly to incorporate air and produce expansion. Generally applied to cream, eggs and gelatin dishes.

APPETIZERS, BEVERAGES

HOW TO MAKE GOOD COFFEE

1. Coffee brands do differ. Try them until you find the one you like best, then stick with it.

2. Choose the correct grind for your coffee maker. Use drip or all-purpose grind for a drip pot, fine grind for a vacuum maker and regular grind for a percolator.

3. Have coffee maker thoroughly clean. Scrub with a light-duty detergent and a soft cloth or sponge after each use, and rinse well.

4. Fresh coffee makes the best. Once opened, store coffee in refrigerator. Store unopened cans in freezer.

5. If possible, use the full capacity of the coffee maker, but never less than half the capacity, for most successful operation.

6. Start with cold fresh water, not water from hot water tap.

7. Use the correct measurement: For each serving, use 2 level measuring-tablespoons (or 1 coffee measure)

and ¾ measuring-cup water. For demitasse coffee, use ½ measuring-cup water.

8. To make the clearest coffee, use a filter or filter paper that fits the coffee basket.

9. Time the brewing accurately. When coffee is over-brewed, undesirable flavors develop.

Drip Method

1. Measure cold water into tea kettle and heat to boiling. Meanwhile, preheat coffeepot by rinsing with very hot water.

2. Measure drip-grind coffee into cone with filter paper or into filter section of coffeepot, depending on the drip pot used.

3. Pour measured freshly boiling water into cone or upper container of drip pot. Cover, depending on pot used.

4. When dripping is completed, in 4 to 6 minutes, remove upper section. Stir and serve.

Vacuum Method

1. Measure fresh cold water into lower bowl. Put on heat and bring to boil. Place filter in upper bowl. When water boils, measure fine-grind coffee into upper bowl.

2. Remove boiling water from heat. Insert upper bowl with slight twist to insure tight seal. Put back over re-duced heat. (When using electric range, turn off electricity.)

3. Most of water will rise into upper bowl. Allow to mix with ground coffee 1 minute, stirring thoroughly in zigzag fashion first 20 seconds.

4. Remove from heat. Brew will return to lower bowl within 2 minutes. Remove upper bowl and serve coffee.

Percolator Method

1. Remove basket and stem and measure cold fresh water into percolator. Put over heat until water boils. Remove from heat.

2. Measure regular-grind coffee into basket.

3. Insert basket and stem in percolator, cover, return to gentle heat and percolate slowly 6 to 8 minutes. (Water level should always be below the bottom of coffee basket.)

4. Remove basket and stem and serve coffee.

For automatic coffee makers, follow manufacturer's directions.

Instant Coffee

Follow directions on label for amount. Pour freshly boiled water over coffee in cups. For a flavor more like freshly brewed coffee, prepare several cups at a time in a pot.

THREE METHODS FOR MAKING
GOOD ICED COFFEE

1. Brew extra breakfast coffee and freeze into coffee ice cubes. Then make iced coffee by pouring regular-strength coffee over the cubes.

2. Make demitasse coffee by using only ½ cup water to each 2 tablespoons coffee. Pour hot over regular ice cubes.

3. Put into a tall glass twice the amount of instant coffee you would use for a cup. Dissolve in a little warm water. Fill glass with ice cubes and cold water.

HOT TEA

Heat teapot by filling it with hot water. Fill teakettle with cold fresh water from tap and bring to full rolling boil. Do not use reheated water. Allow 1 tea bag or 1 teaspoon loose tea for ¾ measuring-cup water and pour water directly over tea in preheated pot. Brew 3 to 5 minutes before serving. If tea is not to be served at once, remove tea bags or loose-tea holder, or strain.

ICED TEA

Make tea as for Hot Tea, above, using 50 percent more tea. Pour tea into ice-filled glasses and serve with lemon and sugar. (Instant tea is handy for making iced tea.)

EGGPLANT MARINARA APPETIZER

1 unpeeled large eggplant
cut in 1" cubes
½ cup white vinegar
(preferably wine vinegar)
1 teaspoon salt

½ teaspoon white pepper
1 clove garlic, minced
1 teaspoon dried oregano
½ teaspoon dried basil
¾ cup olive oil

Boil eggplant in boiling water to cover 8 to 10 minutes. Drain. Cubes should be soft but retain their shape. Mix other ingredients, except oil. Place drained eggplant in large bowl and pour marinade over. Toss thoroughly. Marinate overnight, or at least 8 hours. Before serving, toss with oil. Makes 6 to 8 servings. This will keep about a week in the refrigerator.

TWO-CHEESE APPETIZERS

½ pound (2 cups) Swiss
cheese, grated
½ cup grated Parmesan
cheese
½ cup butter at room
temperature

¾ cup all-purpose flour
¾ cup teaspoon salt
⅛ teaspoon cayenne
⅛ teaspoon nutmeg
1 egg
Paprika

Knead together in bowl 1½ cups Swiss cheese and next 6 ingredients. Form into ball and chill 15 minutes. Divide dough in 6 equal pieces. Shape each piece into a rope 6" long. Put ropes parallel to each other and cut ropes in ½" pieces. Shape each piece into a ball and flatten into a circle about ¼" thick. Arrange on baking sheet, leaving 2" space between. Brush with egg beaten with 1 teaspoon water. Sprinkle each with a little of the remaining Swiss cheese. Bake in hot oven (425°F.) 10 minutes, or until puffed and lightly browned. Cool on rack. Sprinkle with paprika and store in air-tight container. Makes about 6 dozen.

CRAB CANAPÉ

2 cups crab meat	Salt and pepper
¼ cup mayonnaise (about)	24 sautéed small bread
¼ teaspoon Worcestershire	rounds
1 large cucumber	Parsley sprigs

Shred crab meat fine. Mix with enough mayonnaise to hold it together and season with Worcestershire. Peel cucumber and chop very fine. Season lightly with salt and pepper. Spread a thin layer of cucumber on each bread round. Cover with a mound of crab meat. Brown lightly under broiler. Decorate with parsley sprigs before serving. Makes 24 canapés.

TUNA DIP, FINES HERBES

1 can (6-7 ounce) tuna	chives (or 1 teaspoon dried)
1 package (3 ounces) cream cheese	1 teaspoon minced tarragon (or ¼ teaspoon dried)
¼ cup sherry	
2 tablespoons minced parsley	Dairy sour cream
2 tablespoons minced	Salt to taste

Combine all ingredients, adding enough sour cream for dunking consistency. Add 1 or 2 tablespoons of chopped capers or nuts, if desired. Makes about 1 cup.

GUACAMOLE DIP

3 avocados, peeled and mashed
3 tomatoes, peeled, seeded and diced
½ cup minced mild onion
Juice and grated rind of 1 lime
2 tablespoons lemon juice
½ teaspoon salt (coarse if possible)
½ cup mayonnaise
1 cup dairy sour cream
3 dashes hot pepper sauce
Parsley
Cayenne

Blend together all ingredients, except parsley and cayenne. Top with parsley sprigs and dash of cayenne. Serve as a dip for corn chips or potato chips. Makes about 4 cups.

SARDINE DIP

1 package (8 ounces) cream cheese, softened
½ cup dairy sour cream
1 can (4⅜ ounces) skinless and boneless sardines in oil, drained
1 tablespoon minced red or green onion
1 tablespoon lemon juice
¼ teaspoon salt
Paprika

Beat cheese with sour cream and sardines until smooth. Add next 3 ingredients and blend well. Pour into serving dish, sprinkle with paprika and serve with potato chips, crackers or pretzels. Makes about 2 cups.

WINE-PICNIC PÂTÉ

¾ cup butter
1 pound chicken livers
½ pound fresh mushrooms
1 teaspoon salt
⅓ cup finely chopped
  green onions

½ cup dry white wine
1 clove garlic, minced
1/16 teaspoon dillweed
4 drops hot pepper sauce
Pimientos

Melt ¼ cup butter in skillet. Add chicken livers, mushrooms, salt and green onions; simmer 5 minutes. Add wine, garlic, dillweed and hot pepper sauce. Cover and cook slowly 10 minutes, or until chicken livers and mushrooms are very tender. Cool slightly and whirl in a blender until smooth; or press through a sieve. Blend in ½ cup butter. Pack in a crock; chill well. Garnish with pimientos. Makes 3 cups.

MUSHROOM-STUFFED DEVILED EGGS

6 tablespoons ground
  raw mushrooms
2 tablespoons lemon juice
6 eggs, hard-cooked
½ teaspoon salt
Cracked pepper to taste

6 pimiento-stuffed olives,
  chopped
2 tablespoons (about)
  mayonnaise
Parsley sprigs

Sprinkle mushrooms with lemon juice. Mash egg yolks with fork and add seasonings. Mix mushrooms, egg yolks, olives and mayonnaise. Fill egg whites and garnish with sprig of parsley.

TERIYAKI MEATBALLS

Bite-size appetizers baked in Hawaiian sauce.

2 eggs
2 pounds ground
 round steak
½ cup cornflake crumbs
½ cup milk

2 tablespoons grated onion
1 teaspoon salt
¼ teaspoon pepper
Teriyaki sauce

Beat eggs and mix thoroughly with remaining ingredients, except sauce. Shape in balls about 1½″ in diameter and arrange in a layer in shallow baking pan. Pour sauce over balls and bake in slow oven (300°F.) about 45 minutes, turning and basting every 15 minutes. Makes about 3 dozen balls.

Teriyaki Sauce Mix 1 cup soy sauce, ½ cup water, 2 teaspoons ginger juice (or 1 teaspoon powdered ginger), 2 cloves garlic, minced, and 1 teaspoon sugar.

COLD SHRIMPS WITH SPICY SAUCE

3 tablespoons horseradish
1 cup catsup
¼ cup chili sauce
3 tablespoons lemon juice

2 dashes hot pepper sauce
1½ pounds cooked
 cleaned shrimps

Mix all ingredients, except shrimps, and use as a dip or sauce for the shrimps. Makes 6 servings.

RUMAKI

Broil your own appetizers, Japanese style.

⅓ cup soy sauce
2 tablespoons dry sherry
1 clove garlic, minced
⅛ teaspoon pepper
½ pound chicken livers,
   cleaned and cut in half

1 can (5 ounces) water
   chestnuts, drained
About ½ pound bacon,
   each slice halved

Combine first 4 ingredients, pour over chicken livers and marinate 30 minutes. Cut each water chestnut in 3 crosswise slices. Wrap a chicken-liver half and piece of water chestnut together in a half slice of bacon, securing with 1 or 2 toothpicks. Grill over charcoal, turning occasionally, until bacon is crisp. Or put on wire rack set over a shallow pan and bake in hot oven (400°F.) 20 minutes, or until bacon is crisp; do not turn. Makes about 20.

PROSCIUTTO WITH MELON

Cut 1 honeydew melon in half, remove seeds and peel. Cut into individual portions. Serve with rolls of paper-thin prosciutto. (You will need about ¼ pound for 1 melon.) Serve with a pepper mill handy. Makes about 2 dozen.

CHEESY APPETIZERS

⅔ cup grated Parmesan
  cheese
⅓ cup mayonnaise
1 small onion, grated

Dash of Worcestershire
9 slices firm-type bread,
  crusts trimmed

Mix well first 4 ingredients. Cut bread slices in fourths and brown on one side under broiler. Spead untoasted side of each piece with 1 measuring-teaspoonful mixture. Put under broiler until golden brown and serve hot. Makes 3 dozen. Serve on cocktail picks.

SPICED ICED TEA

½ cup sugar
Grated rind and juice of
  1 lemon
Grated rind and juice of
  1 orange

1" cinnamon stick
½ teaspoon whole cloves
4 cups hot double-strength
  tea

Put all ingredients, except last 2, and ½ cup water in small saucepan; bring to boil and simmer, stirring occasionally, 5 minutes. Strain, add to tea and chill. When ready to serve, pour into ice-filled tall glasses. Makes 1½ quarts.

BLENDER VEGETABLE COCKTAIL

Combine in blender 1½ cups tomato juice, 1 stalk celery (cut up), 1 carrot (cut up), 1 teaspoon instant

minced onion, 1 tablespoon lemon juice, ½ teaspoon
Worcestershire and a dash of pepper. Blend and chill.
Serve over ice cubes in glasses. Makes 2 cups.

FRENCH CHOCOLATE

2½ squares unsweetened
   chocolate
½ cup sugar
Dash of salt

½ cup heavy cream,
   whipped
6 cups milk, heated

Put chocolate in heavy saucepan with ½ cup water.
Heat, stirring, until chocolate is melted and blended.
Add sugar and salt and boil, stirring, 4 minutes. Cool
and fold into cream. To serve, put 1 rounded teaspoonful of mixture into each chocolate cup. Add hot milk
to fill cup and stir until chocolate and milk are well
blended. Makes 8 (6-ounce) cups.

SOUPS, ACCOMPANIMENTS

SELECTING A SOUP

Although there are hundreds, possibly thousands of soups, each of them falls into one of three groups:

1. **Thin, clear soups** based on bouillon, consommé or broth. This type is suitable as a first course at dinner.

2. **Thin, light, delicate soups** such as bisques, thin cream soups and vegetable broths. This kind can be served as a first course, or for lunch with a hearty sandwich or salad.

3. **Heavy, thick soups,** including beef or other meat soups, vegetable soups such as minestrone, poultry soups such as mulligatawny, fish soups, chowders and thick cream soups. These are hearty enough to be served as the main course for dinner.

Chilled or jellied soups may fall into any of these three main types. These are, of course, most suitable for hot weather.

PREPARED AND SEMIPREPARED SOUPS

Canned soups are packed in ready-to-serve, condensed and frozen condensed forms. The condensed and frozen condensed soups require the addition of water or milk before heating. These soups, undiluted, also make excellent sauces. Dried soups are of various types. Most contain dehydrated vegetables and some grain produce such as noodles. Bouillon cubes, meat extract, seasoned stock bases and instant bouillon can be used to reinforce the flavor of meat stock for soups and sauces.

GARNISHES FOR SOUPS

Vary the flavor and appearance of a simple soup with one of the following garnishes:
Avocado slices or strips
Whipped cream colored with a little mashed pimiento
Paprika
Chopped fresh herbs
Popcorn

Toasted chopped nuts
Grated cheese
Thin rounds of cooked frankfurter or sausage
Diced fresh tomato
Dairy sour cream
Croutons
Thin lemon slices
Sliced stuffed olives
Crisp bacon bits
Browned onion rings
Paper-thin carrot or radish slices
Thin celery rings
Crisp ready-to-eat cereal
Snipped chives or watercress
Crumbled blue cheese.

SOUP ACCOMPANIMENTS

Try some of the new crackers such as those flavored with bacon, onion or potato; sesame crackers; Swiss- and ham-flavored crackers; vegetable crackers; shredded-wheat wafers; oblong buttery crackers; whole-wheat wafers; round cheese crackers; as well as the old favorites: oyster crackers, saltines, soda crackers, rye wafers, pretzels and pilot crackers. Or try one of the recipes at the end of this chapter.

CHILLED FRUIT SOUP

The fruit: prunes, apricots, raisins, cherries, pears.

½ cup each dried prunes
  and apricots
½ cup seedless raisins
1 stick cinnamon
2 cooking apples, peeled
2 fresh pears

1 can (1 pound) un-
  sweetened sour red
  cherries
1 box cherry-flavored
  gelatin
Lemon slices

In large kettle, soak prunes, apricots and raisins in 3 cups cold water 1 hour. Add cinnamon stick, sliced apples and pears. Cover and simmer 15 minutes, or until fruit is tender. Add undrained cherries and bring to boil. Dissolve gelatin in 1 cup boiling water; stir gently into fruit. Chill overnight. Serve with lemon. Serves 8.

GAZPACHO

1 medium loaf French bread
   (about 1 pound)
2 cloves garlic
1 pound tomatoes, peeled
1 large onion
1 cucumber, peeled
½ cup olive oil

½ cup wine vinegar
Salt and pepper
Croutons
Finely diced cucumber,
   tomato, onion, parsley
   and hard-cooked egg

Cut up bread; soak in water and squeeze almost dry. Put in blender with garlic and coarsely cut tomatoes, onion and cucumber. Blend until thoroughly mixed. Remove cover, put blender on low and add oil gradually. Pour into bowl; stir in vinegar, and salt and pepper to taste. Chill. Serve in large flat bowls. Put croutons and remaining ingredients in individual bowls to be passed at the table. Makes 4 to 6 servings.

TOMATO SHRIMP BISQUE

2 cans (19 ounces each)
   tomatoes
2 cups beef stock or bouillon
1 cup chopped celery and
   leaves
2 onions, sliced
2 carrots, sliced
2 sprigs parsley
4 whole cloves
6 whole black peppercorns
Small piece of bay leaf

Pinch of thyme
2 teaspoons salt
3 tablespoons rice
1½ pounds shrimp, cooked
   and cut up
1 pint light cream
Sherry
Croutons
Thin slices of lemon
Chopped parsley

Put tomatoes, stock, vegetables, seasonings and rice in kettle; bring to boil. Cover and simmer 1 hour. Force through fine sieve or blend smooth in electric blender. Just before serving, add shrimp; heat. Heat cream and add to tomato mixture. Season to taste. Serve at once with sherry and croutons. Garnish with lemon and parsley. Makes about 2½ quarts.

NEW ENGLAND CLAM CHOWDER

18 chowder clams	2 potatoes, diced
1 stalk celery	3 cups milk
¼ pound salt pork, diced	Salt and pepper
2 onions, sliced	6 pilot crackers, crumbled

Scrub clams and put in large kettle with 1 cup water and celery; cover and simmer 15 minutes, or until shells open. Strain off clam broth and reserve. Cook salt pork slowly in heavy kettle until browned. Pour off all but 2 tablespoons fat. Cook onions with pork until tender but not browned. Mince hard part of clams; add to onions and pork with potatoes and clam broth; bring to boil and simmer 20 minutes, or until potatoes are tender. Scald milk; add to soup with soft part of clams; season. Add crackers. Makes 1½ quarts.

MINESTRONE MILANESE

In this northern version of Italy's national soup, rice replaces pasta.

¼ cup olive oil
1 clove garlic, minced
1 onion, minced
1 leek, washed and diced
1 tablespoon chopped parsley
1 teaspoon dried thyme leaves
1 tablespoon tomato paste
3 canned or fresh tomatoes, peeled, seeded and chopped
3 stalks celery, chopped
2 carrots, diced
2 potatoes, diced
¼ small cabbage, shredded
2 zucchinis, diced
Salt to taste
½ teaspoon black pepper
⅓ cup uncooked rice
1 to 1½ cups drained cooked dried beans
Grated Parmesan cheese

Put olive oil in large kettle. Add next 5 ingredients and cook until soft. Add tomato paste thinned with ¼ cup water and cook 5 minutes. Add all remaining ingredients, except rice, beans and cheese, with 1½ quarts hot water or bouillon. Simmer, covered, 1 hour. Bring to boil, add rice and cook until soft. Add beans; heat. Serve with cheese. Makes 3 quarts.

BOUILLABAISSE

1 carrot, diced
2 onions, chopped
2 leeks (white part only)
   or 4 green onions, sliced
1 clove garlic, crushed
½ cup olive oil
3 pounds boned white fish,
   cut in 3" pieces
2 large tomatoes, diced, or
   1 cup canned tomatoes
Salt and pepper
1 bay leaf
2 cups fish stock, clam
   juice or water

1 cup cooked shrimp, crab
   or lobster
2 dozen scrubbed oysters,
   clams or mussels in
   the shell
1 can (4 ounces) pimientos,
   diced
Few shreds of saffron
Juice of 1 lemon
1 cup dry white wine
French bread, sliced
   and toasted
Chopped parsley

Cook first 4 ingredients in oil in large kettle until golden brown. Add fish, tomatoes, salt and pepper, bay leaf and stock. Bring to boil, cover and simmer 20 minutes. Add shellfish and simmer 5 minutes, or until shells open. Add remaining ingredients, except last 2. Heat well. Put toast in tureen and add soup. Sprinkle with parsley. Serves 6 to 8.

UKRAINIAN BORSCH

1 pound beef chuck,
in one piece
8 cups beef broth
Salt and pepper
1 bay leaf
2 tablespoons margarine
1 medium onion, chopped
2 carrots, sliced
1 stalk celery, sliced
4 medium raw beets,
cut in strips

½ medium cabbage (about
1 pound), shredded
4 medium potatoes (about
1 pound), cubed
1 can (6 ounces) tomato
paste
1 tablespoon vinegar
Lemon slices
Dairy sour cream
Chopped dill or parsley
(optional)

Put beef and broth in heavy 4-quart kettle. Add salt
and pepper to taste and the bay leaf. Bring to boil and
skim. Simmer, covered, about 30 minutes. Melt margarine in deep heavy 6-quart kettle or Dutch oven. Add
next 6 ingredients and sauté, stirring, 5 minutes. Add
tomato paste and vinegar and simmer 10 minutes. Remove meat from broth and pour broth over vegetables.
Put meat in kettle with vegetables and simmer, covered,
1½ hours, or until meat is tender. Remove meat and
cut in bite-size pieces. Put back in soup. Add seasoning
to taste. Serve in large soup plates or bowls with a
lemon slice and a tablespoon sour cream in each plate.
Sprinkle lightly with chopped dill, if desired. Makes
about 4 quarts. Leftovers can be frozen.

Note Beef broth can be canned or made out of
bouillon cubes and water. Or cook a leftover ham bone
in water with seasonings, then strain.

FRENCH POTATO SOUP

4 medium potatoes
3 or 4 leeks, white part
  only
Butter or margarine
Salt

1½ cups milk, scalded
White pepper
2 egg yolks
Croutons

Peel and dice potatoes and put in large saucepan. Chop leeks fine and brown lightly in 2 tablespoons butter. Add to potatoes. Add boiling water to cover and ½ teaspoon salt. Cover, bring to boil and cook until potatoes are tender. Purée entire mixture in blender. Add milk and heat. Season to taste and beat in egg yolks. Serve with a spoonful of butter and a few croutons in each bowl. Makes 4 servings.

OYSTER STEW

3 dozen oysters with liquid
½ cup butter or margarine
⅛ teaspoon Worcestershire
Dash of cayenne
½ cup clam juice

4 cups hot milk
4 cups hot light cream
Salt and pepper
Paprika

Cook first 4 ingredients in large skillet just until edges of oysters begin to curl. Add clam juice, milk and cream; heat but do not boil. Add salt and pepper to taste. Sprinkle with paprika. Makes about 2½ quarts. For a simpler stew, allow 2 dozen oysters for every pint of half-and-half (milk and cream). Heat the half-and-half; add the oysters and 1 tablespoon butter for each 2 dozen oysters. Heat and season with salt and pepper.

CHICKEN SOUP WITH SWEDISH DUMPLINGS

1½ quarts chicken broth
2 cups diced cooked chicken
¼ cup flour
1 cup milk
¾ teaspoon salt
2 cardamom seeds, crushed, or ⅛ teaspoon nutmeg
1 tablespoon sugar
2 tablespoons butter
1 egg, beaten
8 blanched almonds, minced
2 sprigs parsley, minced

Bring broth and chicken to boil in kettle. For dumplings, blend flour and a little milk to a smooth paste in saucepan. Add remaining milk, salt, cardamom and sugar. Cook until thickened, stirring constantly. Add butter and stir until melted. Pour over egg, mix and cool. Add almonds and parsley. Drop into gently boiling soup. Cook 2 minutes, or until dumplings rise to top. Makes 4 servings.

SCOTCH BARLEY BROTH

2 pounds lamb neck or breast
½ cup pearl barley
Salt
6 whole black peppercorns
¾ cup each chopped onion and celery
¾ cup each diced yellow turnip and carrot
1 carrot, grated
1 leek, sliced
1 cup cooked peas
2 tablespoons minced parsley
Pepper

Put lamb, barley, 1 teaspoon salt and the pepper-corns in a large heavy pan; add 2 quarts water. Simmer about 1½ hours. Cool; skim. Remove meat, trim off fat and bones and dice meat; put meat back in soup. Add onion, celery, turnip and diced carrot. Bring to a boil and simmer 30 minutes, or until vegetables are tender. Add remaining ingredients and season to taste. Heat through. Makes 1½ quarts.

CROUTONS

Trim crusts from bread slices and dice bread. Sauté in butter until an even brown. Or butter slices of trimmed bread, cut in dice and brown in moderate oven.

CARAWAY CHEESE STICKS

½ cup butter
2½ cups sifted flour
¾ cup grated Swiss cheese
½ teaspoon salt
½ cup milk

2 teaspoons baking powder
½ teaspoon curry powder
2 eggs
Caraway seed
Coarse salt

Cut butter into flour and cheese. Add next 4 ingredients and 1 egg; mix until blended. Let rest for 1 hour. On lightly floured board, roll to ¼" thickness. Cut in strips 4" x 1". Beat remaining egg. Brush each bar with egg and sprinkle with caraway seed and salt. Bake in hot oven (425°F.) 10 to 12 minutes. Store airtight. Makes about 4½ dozen.

Poppy-seed Cheese Sticks Follow above recipe, substituting poppy seed for the caraway seed.

BEEF

HOW TO BUY BEEF

America's favorite meat, beef is guaranteed as to wholesomeness and graded as to tenderness by government inspectors: the purple "U. S. Inspected and Passed" stamp on the individual cut indicates that it measures up to health standards. And many beef cuts also carry the shield-shaped purple U. S. D. A. grade stamp to indicate quality. The grades of beef are:

U. S. D. A. Prime Highest grade, but most of this beef goes to restaurants and hotels so is not widely available to the housewife.

U. S. D. A. Choice Highest grade commonly found in retail stores. This grade is well-marbled meat, tender and juicy. The lean is usually bright red, firm and velvety to the touch. It is well streaked with little veins of fat and has a thick, white or creamy white, firm fat covering. The meat is especially flavorsome and tender. Top Choice is the best meat of this grade.

U. S. D. A. Good has slightly less marbling, meat is slightly darker red and fat covering is somewhat thinner than that found in U. S. D. A. Choice.

Amount to Buy

• Buy ¼ to ⅓ pound per serving for boneless cuts such as ground beef, boneless stew, boned roasts and steaks, flank and variety meats.

• Buy ½ to ¾ pound per serving for cuts with some bone such as rib roast, unboned steak.

• Buy ¾ to 1 pound per serving for bony and fatty cuts such as short ribs, plate, brisket.

Keeping Times for Raw Beef

Remove or loosen wrapper and store unwrapped in meat container or loosely wrapped in coldest part of refrigerator.

Refrigerator shelf
Ground beef: 1 day
Stew meat, cut up: 2 days
Steak: 2 to 4 days
Roasts: 3 to 6 days

Refrigerator frozen-food compartment, prepared for freezing
Ground beef: 2 to 4 days
Other cuts: 1 week

Freezer, prepared for freezing
Wrap closely and seal tightly in moisture-vapor-

proof material and freeze quickly. Store at 0°F., or lower, a maximum of 3 to 4 months for ground beef and 6 to 8 months for other beef.

Keeping Times for Cooked Beef

To keep cooked beef and gravy, cool quickly, cover tightly and put in coldest part of refrigerator. Prepared for freezing, it may be kept 4 to 5 days in refrigerator frozen-food compartment. When stored in freezer, use within 2 to 3 months.

COOKING BEEF

• Use dry heat for the more tender cuts of beef. This method includes roasting, broiling, grilling, deep-fat frying, pan-frying.
• Use moist heat for the less tender cuts of beef. This method includes braising, pot-roasting, stewing and fricasseeing.
• Marinades with tomatoes and vinegar are often helpful as tenderizers. Commercial meat tenderizers may also be used, following manufacturer's directions.

FLANK STEAK TERIYAKI BARBECUE

¾ cup vegetable oil
¼ cup each soy sauce and honey
2 tablespoons each vinegar and finely chopped green onions
1 large clove garlic, minced
1½ teaspoons ground ginger
1 flank steak (about 1½ pounds) (not scored)

Combine all ingredients except meat. Pour over flank steak and marinate 4 hours or more; turn occasionally. Broil under high heat, 2″ from heat, or grill steak over hot coals, turning once, until done as desired, about 5 minutes each side for medium rare. Baste occasionally with marinade. Carve in thin slices, cutting diagonally across the grain from top to bottom of steak. Makes 4 servings.

BEEF STROGANOFF

2 pounds lean sirloin steak
3 tablespoons sweet butter
2 onions, thinly sliced
1 pound mushrooms, sliced
1 tablespoon flour
¼ teaspoon white pepper
½ teaspoon paprika

Dash of cayenne
1 cup dairy sour cream
Hot buttered noodles,
  seasoned with poppy
  seed
Chopped chives or dill

With sharp knife, cut beef across grain into narrow strips. Heat 2 tablespoons butter in large heavy skillet and add meat and onions. Cook over high heat a few minutes, turning meat to brown all sides. Reduce heat, add mushrooms and cook, covered, 10 minutes longer. Remove mixture to top of double boiler or chafing dish and put over hot water to keep warm. To juices in skillet, add remaining butter and blend in flour and seasonings. Gradually add sour cream, blending to keep smooth. Add to meat. Serve with noodles and a sprinkling of chives. Serves 6.

STEAK AU POIVRE

Crush coarsely 1½ tablespoons peppercorns (crushed, coarse ground or seasoned pepper may be substituted in lesser amounts). Press pepper firmly into both sides of a 2″-thick top sirloin steak, using heel of hand. Let the steak stand for half to three quarters of an hour. Now grill it over a medium fire for 6 to 8 minutes on each side or broil 2″ below high heat. Remove the steak to a hot platter, sprinkle with salt and place a large chunk of sweet butter on top. Let this melt and run over the surface before carving. Or flame it with Cognac before serving. Serve with boiled new potatoes rolled in butter and minced tarragon.

BEEF WITH BROCCOLI

1 pound flank or other steak, cut in ¼″ slices about 2″ long	1 teaspoon sugar
	½ bunch broccoli
	5 tablespoons vegetable oil
¼ cup soy sauce	½ teaspoon salt
1 tablespoon cornstarch	1 slice gingerroot or
1 tablespoon dry sherry	¼ cup sliced onion

Mix first 6 ingredients and set aside. Cut broccoli in florets about 2″ long, peel stalk and slice in 2″ lengths less than ½″ thick. Put 2 tablespoons oil in hot skillet over high heat. Add salt and broccoli and stir-fry, turning constantly, until broccoli is dark green—not over 2 minutes. Remove from skillet. Put remaining oil in skillet and add ginger and beef mixture. Stir-fry, turning constantly, not more than 2 minutes. Add broccoli and mix well. Serve at once. Makes 2 or 3 servings.

Note Broccoli tends to make oil spatter, so drain thoroughly after washing. Precooked broccoli can also be used.

BAVARIAN BEEF STEW

1½ pounds round steak, cubed
2 medium onions, sliced
3 tablespoons butter or margarine
1 bay leaf
1½ teaspoons salt
¼ teaspoon pepper
1 teaspoon caraway seed
¼ cup vinegar
1 small head cabbage, cut in wedges
¼ cup finely crushed gingersnaps

Brown beef and onion in butter. Add 3 cups boiling water, seasonings and seed. Bring to boil, cover and simmer 1½ to 2 hours. Add vinegar and cabbage. Cover and simmer about 45 minutes. Remove cabbage and arrange around edge of platter. Pile meat in center. Soften gingersnap crumbs in ¼ cup warm water and stir into gravy. Add additional vinegar and seasonings if necessary. Pour over meat. Makes 6 servings.

BEEF À LA MODE

4 pounds beef for pot roast
Salt and pepper
2 cups dry white wine
(Sauterne or Chablis)
2 tablespoons each fat
and flour
2 cups meat stock
1 cup canned tomatoes

1 clove garlic
Few sprigs of parsley
2 stalks celery
1 bay leaf
⅛ teaspoon thyme
6 carrots, cut in pieces
3 onions, quartered

Season meat with salt and pepper. Put in bowl and pour wine over top. Let stand in refrigerator 5 to 6 hours, turning occasionally. Then remove from wine and wipe dry. Brown on all sides in hot fat. Remove meat and pour off fat. Brown flour in kettle. Add meat, marinade and remaining ingredients, except last 2. Bring to boil, cover and simmer about 2 hours. Remove meat and skim off fat. Return meat to kettle with vegetables. Cover and simmer 1½ to 2 hours longer, or until meat and vegetables are tender. Then remove the meat and vegetables to a heated platter and season gravy with salt and pepper to taste. Makes about 6 servings.

LEMON POT ROAST

1 clove garlic, minced
¼ cup lemon juice
3 slices lemon, cut in
quarters
1 small onion, chopped
½ teaspoon each seasoned

salt, celery salt and
pepper
¼ teaspoon marjoram
3 pounds lean boneless
chuck

Mix ¼ cup water with all ingredients, except meat, and refrigerate 24 hours. Brown meat in greased kettle and add sauce. Cover and simmer about 3 hours. Makes 6 to 8 servings.

GLAZED BEEF BRISKET

First-cut fresh boneless beef
   brisket, about 4 pounds
1 tablespoon peppercorns
2½ teaspoons salt
⅛ teaspoon ground allspice
2 tablespoons fine dry bread
   crumbs

1 teaspoon garlic salt
1 onion, sliced
Glaze
Carrot slices
Green-pepper strips

Wipe meat with damp cloth and put on board. With dull side of heavy knife, pound meat well on both sides. Then score inside of meat lengthwise and crosswise, making scorings about ½″ apart. Put peppercorns in small cloth bag and crush with hammer or mallet. Sprinkle scored side of meat with the pepper, 1½ teaspoons salt and next 3 ingredients. Roll up tightly lengthwise (the right way for slicing across the grain). Tie firmly in several places with string and put in large heavy kettle. Add onion and remaining salt. Cover with hot water. Bring to boil, cover and simmer 3 hours, or until tender. Chill thoroughly in the broth. Put on serving platter and remove string. Spoon some Glaze over meat to cover. Refrigerate about 10 minutes. Pour remaining Glaze over meat to cover well, letting mixture run onto platter. (If gelatin congeals, set in pan of warm water a few seconds.) Decorate meat with carrot slices and green-pepper strips. Chill until serving time, then dice gelatin on platter and slice meat. Makes 8 servings.

Glaze Soften 1 envelope unflavored gelatin in ¼ cup cold water. Heat 1 can (10½ ounces) beef consommé with ½ cup water. Add gelatin and stir until dissolved. Chill until cold but not set.

POT AU FEU

(Boiled Beef with Vegetables)

5 pounds cross rib, short rib or brisket of beef	1 bay leaf
1½ pounds salt pork	1 teaspoon thyme
1 marrow bone	2 or 3 sprigs parsley
10 medium onions, peeled	1 teaspoon salt
4 whole cloves	¼ teaspoon pepper
9 leeks, well washed	8 small turnips, peeled
10 carrots, peeled and sliced	1 medium cabbage, cut in quarters or sixths

Put meat, salt pork, marrow bone, 2 onions stuck with cloves, 3 leeks, 2 carrots and the herbs in heavy kettle. Add water to cover 1½" above meat. Bring to boil and boil rapidly 5 minutes. Skim off any scum that forms on top, add salt and pepper and cover kettle. Lower heat and simmer 2 to 2½ hours, or until meat is tender. Remove meat and keep warm. Add remaining vegetables, except cabbage, and cook until done. Add cabbage the last 12 minutes. Cut salt pork and beef in slices and arrange on a hot platter. Surround meat with vegetables and garnish with marrow from marrow bone. Coarse salt, mustard and horseradish are traditional with this dish. Potatoes cooked in jackets and good

pickles are also a nice addition. Taste broth for seasoning, pour into bowls and serve separately. Makes 8
servings.

BARBECUED SHORT RIBS

3 pounds short ribs of beef
1 onion, chopped
½ cup sliced celery
2 tablespoons
  Worcestershire
1 teaspoon prepared
  mustard
1½ teaspoons salt
⅛ teaspoon pepper

Brown short ribs on all sides in heavy kettle; pour off
fat. Add ½ cup water, vegetables and seasonings.
Cover and simmer 2 hours, or until tender, turning
meat several times and adding more water if necessary.
Makes 4 servings.

BEEF AND VEGETABLE PIE

2½ pounds boneless
  beef chuck
6 tablespoons all-purpose
  flour
2 teaspoons salt
¼ teaspoon pepper
3 tablespoons margarine
  or other fat
2 onions, sliced
1 teaspoon steak sauce
1 teaspoon seasoned salt
1 can (1 pound) tomatoes
2 carrots, sliced
3 cups sliced potato
1 box or 1 stick pastry mix

Cut beef in 1" cubes and dredge with 3 tablespoons
flour seasoned with the salt and pepper. Brown on all
sides in the margarine in heavy kettle. Add onions and

brown lightly. Add 2 cups water, the steak sauce and seasoned salt. Bring to boil, cover and simmer 1 hour, or until meat is almost tender. Add tomatoes, carrots and potato. Simmer, covered, ½ hour longer. Blend remaining flour with a little cold water and stir into mixture. Cook, stirring gently, until thickened. Pour into 3-quart casserole. Prepare pastry mix as directed on the label. Roll out to fit top of casserole, trim edges and flute. Prick top to allow steam to escape. Bake in hot oven (425°F.) 25 minutes, or until top is browned. Makes 8 servings.

HUNGARIAN GOULASH

3 pounds boneless beef chuck or 3½ pounds bone-in chuck	1 tablespoon salt
	½ teaspoon black pepper
	Paprika
3 pounds large onions, cut in wedge-shaped pieces (about 7 cups)	Parsley
	Cooked noodles
	Dairy sour cream

Cut meat in 1" cubes, discarding any excess fat and bone. Put meat, onion, salt, pepper and 2 tablespoons paprika in large heavy kettle or Dutch oven. Cook over medium heat about 20 minutes, stirring often. Cover and simmer 2 hours, stirring occasionally. Uncover and simmer until liquid cooks down to gravy consistency. Garnish with parsley and serve with noodles and a generous dollop of sour cream sprinkled with paprika. Makes 6 servings.

CHILI CON CARNE

1 cup dried pinto beans	1 teaspoon crushed
3 pounds lean stew beef	cumin seed
¼ cup olive oil	1 teaspoon oregano
1 bay leaf	3 tablespoons paprika
2 tablespoons chili powder	3 tablespoons cornmeal
1 tablespoon salt	1 tablespoon flour
4 cloves garlic, minced	

Cover washed beans with 4 cups water, bring to boil and boil 2 minutes. Cover and let stand 1 hour, then cook until tender. Drain. Cut meat in ½" cubes and sear in hot oil. Add 6 cups water, cover, bring to boil and simmer 1 hour. Add bay leaf and next 6 ingredients. Simmer ½ hour. Blend cornmeal, flour and cold water to make a paste. Stir into mixture; simmer 5 minutes. Add beans and heat. Makes 6 servings.

NEW ENGLAND BOILED DINNER

4- to 5-pound corned beef	6 medium carrots, peeled
brisket	8 medium potatoes, peeled
6 small beets, unpeeled	1 small cabbage, quartered
6 small white turnips,	Vinegar
unpeeled	Prepared mustard

Wash beef and put in large kettle. Cover with cold water. Bring to boil, cover and simmer 4 to 4½ hours, or until tender. Remove meat from kettle. Put beets in saucepan and add some of the broth from the corned beef. Cover and simmer until tender. Add turnips, carrots and potatoes to broth in kettle. Cover and simmer 20 minutes, or until tender. Add cabbage and simmer

15 minutes longer. Remove vegetables and keep hot. Put meat back in broth a few minutes to reheat. Slip skins off beets. Slice beef and arrange in center of hot platter. Surround with the vegetables and serve with vinegar and mustard. Makes 6 servings with meat left over.

RED-FLANNEL HASH

2 cups chopped cooked
  corned beef
2 cups chopped cooked
  beets
4 cups chopped cooked
  potato

1 large onion, chopped
Salt and pepper to taste
Light cream
¼ cup bacon or pork
  drippings

Combine beef with beets, potato, onion, seasonings and enough cream to bind mixture. Heat drippings in large skillet. Spoon meat mixture into skillet and spread evenly in pan. Cook over low heat, without stirring, until the bottom is well crusted. Fold as for omelet. Makes 4 to 6 servings.

LAMB, VEAL, VARIETY MEATS

HOW TO BUY LAMB

Wholesome lamb carries the Federal stamp "U. S. Inspected and Passed." It may also have a stamp indicating the quality grade. Grades are Prime, Choice and Good.

A clear clue to the quality of lamb is the color of the uncooked lean meat, which varies with the age of the animal. Young, milk-fed lamb will have light pink lean. Spring lamb (under one year of age) will have deeper pink lean and the average market lamb will have a pinkish-red lean. The texture should always be fine and velvety. The fat should be smooth, firm, white, rather brittle but of a waxy consistency. The outer fat is covered with a parchment-like tissue called the fell, which helps keep the wholesale cut fresh and protected if the lamb is aged. This is sometimes removed from retail cuts before they are offered for sale.

For lamb for a small family, a practical way to use a leg of lamb is to have it divided into three types of cuts: chops cut from the loin end, a roast from the center, and the meat from the lower leg cut for stewing.

HOW TO BUY VEAL

Veal is beef less than three months old. The inspecting and stamping system is the same as for lamb. The color of lean veal, like lamb, varies with the age of the animal, becoming redder with increasing age. The lean portions of young, milk-fed veal will be grayish-pink. The texture should be fine and velvety.

STORAGE OF LAMB AND VEAL

Keep in the coldest part of the refrigerator, loosely wrapped in waxed paper. Use chops or steaks within 2 to 3 days. Roasts can be kept a little longer, but use ground meat within 24 hours of purchase.

VARIETY MEATS

Variety or organ meats include sweetbreads, liver, kidneys, brains, heart and tongue and are more perishable than the muscle meats. They must be absolutely fresh, firm to the touch and sweet in odor when purchased. They should be kept in coldest part of refrigerator not longer than 2 days. Cooked, these meats can be stored in refrigerator 1 to 2 days.

STUFFED LAMB CHOPS

Add a little horseradish or a dash of vinegar to the tomato sauce.

6 thick loin lamb chops
2 tablespoons minced onion
1 tablespoon butter
2 tablespoons minced celery
2 tablespoons fresh
white-bread crumbs
1 teaspoon grated
lemon rind
1 tablespoon chopped
parsley or chives
Salt and pepper
1 egg yolk
Tomato sauce

Cut a pocket in chops. Cook onion in butter until soft and golden. Combine with all other ingredients, except last 2. Moisten with egg yolk. Stuff chops and broil as usual. Serve with hot sauce. Makes 6 servings.

BUTTERFLIED LEG OF LAMB

Barbecue outdoors a leg of lamb that's been boned and opened out.

Place butterflied leg of lamb (5 to 6 pounds before boning) on grill, fat side up, over medium coals. Cook 50 to 60 minutes, basting frequently with Wine Sauce and turning occasionally. To carve, start at one end and cut across the grain into thin slices. Makes 8 servings.

Wine Sauce

1 teaspoon salt	1 cup each dry wine and
¼ teaspoon ground ginger	beef or chicken stock
1 tablespoon each instant	2 tablespoons each orange
minced onion, dried	marmalade and wine
rosemary and marjoram	vinegar
1 large bay leaf, crumbled	

Combine all ingredients in a saucepan; simmer 20 minutes, stirring occasionally. Brush over lamb before and during grilling.

Cheesed Barbecued Lamb Slices Rub surface of butterflied leg of lamb with salt, pepper and ¼ teaspoon ground cumin. Grill as directed, basting occasionally with simple French dressing. Carve lamb in very thin slices. Top each one with a thin slice of Muenster cheese, using about 1 pound. Arrange overlapping on platter; sprinkle with more cumin.

SWEDISH COFFEE-BASTED ROAST LAMB

Leg of lamb (5 to 6 pounds)	2 tablespoons sugar
Salt and pepper	2 tablespoons flour
1 cup strong hot coffee	Red currant jelly
¼ cup light cream	

Rub lamb with salt and pepper. Roast as usual, basting during last hour with coffee mixed with cream and sugar. Make gravy from pan drippings: Skim off excess fat. Lightly brown flour. Mix with cold water to a thin paste; stir into drippings, beating well. Add water as needed for gravy consistency, simmering until thick and smooth. Check seasoning. To each cup of gravy add 1 tablespoon currant jelly; heat and stir until jelly melts. Serve with lamb. Makes 8 servings.

SHISH KEBAB

2 pounds boneless shoulder or leg of lamb
1 cup dry red wine
3 tab'espoons red-wine vinegar
½ cup olive oil
1 clove garlic, crushed
1 large onion, sliced
Bay leaf, thyme, cumin,

oregano, or marjoram as desired
Whole boiled small onions
Whole small or quartered tomatoes
Green-pepper chunks
Cubes of eggplant or zucchini

Cut lamb in 1" cubes. Marinate 24 hours in mixture of next 5 ingredients and seasonings as desired; turn cubes occasionally. String meat on skewers, alternating with pieces of vegetable. Broil to desired doneness over charcoal fire or cook in broiler, basting occasionally with the marinade. Makes 4 servings.

SAVORY TURKISH LAMB PILAF

½ pound boneless lamb, cut in julienne strips
¼ cup butter
3 medium onions, chopped fine
¼ cup pine nuts or walnut pieces
2 cups uncooked rice
1 large fresh tomato, peeled, seeded and chopped
¼ cup currants or chopped seedless raisins
2 teaspoons salt
1 teaspoon pepper
½ teaspoon ground sage
¼ teaspoon allspice
4 cups boiling-hot bouillon
Chopped parsley or mint (optional)

Sauté lamb strips in butter until golden brown. Remove and keep hot. In the same pan cook onion until soft but not brown; add nuts and rice and cook over medium heat 5 minutes, stirring constantly. Add next 7 ingredients; stir thoroughly. Cover tightly. Cook over lowest possible heat until rice is tender and liquid absorbed, about 20 to 30 minutes. Return lamb strips to rice and heat through. Remove from heat. Cover and stand in warm place for about 15 minutes. Sprinkle with 1 to 2 tablespoons parsley or mint, if desired. Makes 6 to 8 servings.

VEAL AND PEPPERS, ITALIAN STYLE

Serve it on hot cooked rice, macaroni or spaghetti.

1½ pounds boneless lean
   veal
3 tablespoons olive oil
2 green peppers, cut in
   eighths

1 can (3 ounces) sliced
   mushrooms
Pinch of crushed red pepper
2 cans (8 ounces each)
   tomato sauce
Salt and pepper to taste

Cut meat in bite-size pieces. Brown on all sides in hot oil in skillet. Add green pepper, cover, reduce heat and cook 10 minutes, stirring occasionally. Add remaining ingredients. Simmer, covered, 30 minutes longer, or until tender. Serves 4.

VEAL STEW MARENGO

2½ pounds breast of veal
Salt and pepper
6 medium onions, sliced
2 tablespoons butter
2 tablespoons vegetable oil
¼ cup flour
1 can (29 ounces) tomatoes,
   drained and cut in large
   pieces
1 cup dry white wine
1 cup consomme or bouillon

1 clove garlic, minced
⅛ teaspoon each thyme and
   marjoram
1 bay leaf
Few sprigs of parsley,
   chopped
1 can (4 ounces) sliced
   mushrooms, drained
Boiled potatoes, rice or
   noodles

Cut meat in 1½" cubes. Season and brown with

onion in hot butter and oil in large skillet. Blend in flour; add all ingredients, except last 2. Bring to boil, cover and simmer 45 minutes. Add mushrooms and simmer 15 minutes longer. Serve with potatoes. Makes 4 to 6 servings.

VEAL SCALLOPS MILANESE

An Italian scallopini dish from the town of Milan.

Cover 1½ pounds thin veal scallops with milk; soak 1 hour. Drain milk from veal and add to 2 beaten eggs. Dip scallops in flour, then in egg-milk mixture and then in ⅔ cup fine dry crumbs. Heat 6 tablespoons butter in skillet until bubbly. Sauté veal pieces until tender and browned on both sides. Drain on absorbent paper. Season to taste with salt and freshly ground black pepper. Makes 4 servings.

Veal Scallops Parmesan Add to fine dry bread crumbs used in dipping scallops: ½ cup grated Parmesan, ⅓ cup chopped parsley and 1 tablespoon fresh basil or 1 teaspoon dried basil. After veal is cooked and removed to hot platter, rinse skillet with ½ cup white wine, scraping browned bits from bottom. Pour over scallops.

BLINDE VINKEN

(Stuffed Veal Birds)

A variation of the traditional Dutch recipe.

8 slices leg of veal, about
   3" x 4" x ½"
4 slices bread, crumbled
½ cup milk
1 small onion, finely
   chopped
2 ounces (or more) sausage
   meat

Salt and freshly ground
   pepper
2 eggs
8 thin slices bacon
1 dill pickle, cut in 8 slivers
Fine dry bread crumbs
3 tablespoons each
   vegetable oil and butter
½ cup light cream

Pound veal to ¼" thickness. For stuffing, mix next 4 ingredients with 1 teaspoon salt and a dash of pepper. Separate one egg; brush white over each piece of veal. Place a piece of bacon and a sliver of pickle on each veal slice; spread with 1 tablespoon stuffing. Roll and secure with small skewers or toothpicks. Beat slightly the remaining egg yolk and whole egg. Dip each veal bird in the egg mixture, then roll in crumbs. Chill ½ hour. When ready to cook, heat oil and butter in skillet and brown the birds well on all sides. Add ½ cup boiling water, cover and simmer 20 minutes. Remove birds to a hot platter. Add cream and cook down 1 minute. Correct the seasoning and pour over veal birds. These are especially good with mashed potatoes. Makes 4 servings.

OXTAIL STEW

Cut 2 oxtails in pieces and dredge with ½ cup all-purpose flour. Brown on all sides in 2 tablespoons vegetable oil in large kettle. Add 2 quarts water, 1 teaspoon salt, ¼ teaspoon whole black peppercorns, dash of cayenne and 1 bay leaf. Bring to boil, skim, cover and simmer 3 hours. Remove oxtails, strain broth, cool and remove fat. Separate meat from bones. To broth and meat add ½ cup diced celery, 1 chopped leek or onion and 1 diced carrot. Bring to boil and simmer 30 minutes. Add ½ cup tomato purée, 1 teaspoon steak sauce, few sprigs of chopped parsley, salt and pepper. Simmer 10 minutes longer. Brown 2 tablespoons flour; blend in 1 tablespoon butter. Add to stew and bring to boil. Makes 4 to 6 servings.

LIVER-BACON-POTATO CASSEROLE

1 pound sliced bacon
2 medium onions, sliced
1 pound liver, sliced (any kind)
1 tablespoon butter or margarine
1 tablespoon flour
1 cup milk
1 teaspoon prepared mustard

1 teaspoon Worcestershire
2 teaspoons prepared horseradish
½ teaspoon salt
⅛ teaspoon pepper
1 box (1 pound) frozen potatoes for hashed browns
½ cup grated sharp Cheddar cheese

Cook bacon until crisp. Remove from skillet, drain and crumble. Pour off most of fat. Add onion to skillet and sauté until golden. Push aside, add liver and cook

until browned and done. Remove liver and cut in cubes.
Melt butter in saucepan and blend in flour. Gradually
add milk and cook, stirring, until thickened. Add next 5
ingredients. Put liver, onion, potato and 1 cup crumbled
bacon in shallow 1½-quart casserole. Add sauce and
mix well. Mix remaining bacon and cheese and sprinkle
on top. Bake in moderate oven (350°F.) about 30
minutes. Makes 6 servings.

Note If desired, 4 cups diced cold cooked potatoes
can be substituted for hashed browns.

STEAK-KIDNEY CASSEROLE

2 beef kidneys
1 pound round steak, cut
  ½" thick
Flour
1 onion, minced
2 tablespoons margarine
Salt and pepper
1 bay leaf
Few sprigs parsley

Few celery leaves
½ pound mushrooms, sliced
2 teaspoons steak sauce
Dash of hot pepper sauce
Pastry (recipe made with
  1½ cups flour) or 1 box
  (10 ounces) pie-crust mix
1 egg

Remove outer membrane of kidneys. Split kidneys
open and remove all fat and white veins. Soak in cold
water to cover 30 minutes. Drain and cut kidneys and
steak in 1" pieces. Dredge with flour and brown with
onion in the margarine in kettle or Dutch oven. Sprinkle
with 2 teaspoons salt and ¼ teaspoon pepper. Add next
4 ingredients and 2 cups water. Bring to boil, cover and
simmer 1 hour, or until meats are tender. Then thicken
with 2 to 3 tablespoons flour blended with a little cold
water. Add remaining seasonings, and salt and pepper
to taste. Pour into 1½-quart casserole. Roll pastry to

fit top and arrange on casserole; trim and flute edges with fork. Brush with egg beaten with 1 teaspoon cold water. From remaining pastry, cut leaf and stem designs and arrange on pastry. Brush with egg mixture. Bake in very hot oven (450°F.) about 20 minutes. Makes 6 servings.

SMOKED TONGUE DINNER

1 smoked beef tongue
  (3 to 3½ pounds)
1 onion, sliced
1 stalk celery
1 bay leaf

½ teaspoon whole black
  peppercorns
6 whole onions
6 carrots, cut in quarters
1½ pounds whole green
  beans

Put tongue in kettle and cover with water. Add next 4 ingredients. Bring to boil, cover and simmer 3 to 3½ hours, or until tongue is tender. Remove tongue; pull off skin and remove bones. Add remaining ingredients to kettle. Slice tongue, arrange on top. Cook ½ hour, or until vegetables are tender.

MUSHROOMS AND SWEETBREADS

2 pairs sweetbreads
2 tablespoons lemon juice
  or vinegar
Salt
½ pound mushrooms, sliced
¼ cup butter or margarine
¼ cup flour
1 cup chicken broth or
  bouillon

½ cup cream or milk
Dash of cayenne
¼ teaspoon mace or nutmeg
¼ teaspoon pepper
Soft bread crumbs
Grated Cheddar cheese
Toast points

Plunge sweetbreads into cold water and let stand about ½ hour. Drain and cover with boiling water. Add lemon juice and a little salt and bring to boil; cover and simmer about 20 minutes. Drain and rinse with cold water. Remove membrane and tubes. Cut sweetbreads in ½″ pieces. Sauté mushrooms in butter 2 to 3 minutes. Remove mushrooms and blend flour into drippings in skillet. Gradually add chicken broth and cream. Cook, stirring, until thickened and smooth. Add sweetbreads, mushrooms, 1 teaspoon salt and the other seasonings. Put in shallow 1½-quart baking dish. Sprinkle lightly with bread crumbs and grated cheese. Bake in moderate oven (375°F.) 30 minutes, or until browned on top. Serve on toast. Serves 6.

PORK, SAUSAGE, FRANKFURTERS

HOW TO BUY FRESH PORK

Wholesome pork carries the Federal stamp "U. S. Inspected and Passed," but is not graded for quality federally. For flavorful, tender and juicy results, choose pork that is fine and velvety in texture and is well-marbled with fat or has generous amounts of intramuscular fat. Dark meat is less acidic, juicier, and shrinks less in cooking.

FRESH-PORK STORAGE

Unless you select your pork from the prepacked counter, remove the butcher's wrapping and cover loosely. Prepackaged pork can be left in its original wrappings. Put pork promptly in the coldest part of the refrigerator and use within 1 to 2 days.

COOKING CAUTION

Whatever method is used, pork should always be cooked until well done. Prolonged heat kills any trichina organisms sometimes present in this meat.

HOW TO BUY SMOKED HAM

Kinds of Ham

Two kinds of ham are generally available—**fully-cooked** or **cook-before-eating hams.** A third kind, the so-called **country-style ham,** is not sold in all localities. Country-style hams are heavily cured and firm-textured. They require soaking and simmering in water before baking. Hams are labeled so that it's easy to tell which kind you are buying.

Styles of Ham

Hams are available in several styles: bone-in; skinless, shankless (shank removed, meat skinned and trimmed of excess fat); semi-boneless; boneless; boneless-skinless (ham rolls); and canned ham, also boneless and skinless. All come in various sizes.

HAM STORAGE

Refrigerate hams at 40°F. or less. Like all meats, ham is at its best when used promptly. Freezing tends to reduce the flavor.

KINDS OF SAUSAGES

Southern European Sausages

In this group dry sausages predominate because in the warm Mediterranean area, when methods of refrigeration were very primitive, preserving meat in summer was a great problem. Some Italian varieties are: salami, pepperoni, Italian sweet, Italian hot, and bologna.

Northern European Sausages

The cooler climate of northern Europe produced mainly fresh and cooked sausages. From Germany come *bockwurst,* bratwurst, fresh Thüringer, mettwurst, frankfurters, *knoblauch,* knackwurst, Berliner sausage, blood sausage, liverwurst, and cervelat. Austria contributed Vienna sausage; Sweden, Göteborg.

American Sausages

America's gifts to the sausage world are fresh and smoked country-style pork sausage, in bulk and link form and brown-and-serve links. But because immigrants from Europe brought their favorite recipes with them, Americans today can enjoy most European varieties.

KINDS OF FRANKFURTERS

Frankfurters range from large dinner franks to tiny cocktail size and may be skinless or in natural casings. Ingredients are listed on packages in descending order of weight. If name is simply "Frankfurters," "Wieners" or "Hot Dogs," approved fillers such as milk powder and soy flour may be present in limited quantities. Frankfurters labeled "All Meat" must contain meat only. "All Beef" means just that. The latter may also be labeled "Kosher." Frankfurter seasonings may include coriander, garlic, mustard, nutmeg, salt, sugar and white pepper.

STORAGE

Frankfurters can be kept refrigerated in their original wrappers about 2 weeks. They can be frozen 1 to 2 months.

GLAZED ROAST FRESH HAM

1 fresh ham, 10 to 12 pounds
Salt and pepper
⅓ cup dark corn syrup
1 tablespoon soy sauce
¼ teaspoon ginger
1 tablespoon cornstarch
Halved pineapple rings
Preserved kumquats
Orange wedges
Parsley

Put ham, fat side up, on rack in roasting pan. Sprinkle with salt and pepper and insert meat thermometer into center of thickest muscle. Roast in slow oven (325°F.) 5 to 6 hours, or until thermometer registers 185°F. About ½ hour before meat is done, cover with mixture of corn syrup and next 3 ingredients. Continue roasting until well glazed. Remove to hot platter. Garnish with remaining ingredients. Makes 10 to 12 servings.

ROAST PORK, SPANISH STYLE

Make a paste of ¼ teaspoon each powdered sage and ginger, 1 crushed garlic clove, 1 teaspoon each salt and flour, and sherry to moisten. Spread on fat side of 4-pound pork loin. Bake on rack in roasting pan in moderate oven (325°F.) 3 hours, or until meat thermometer registers 185°F., basting frequently with additional sherry during the roasting. Make gravy with drippings in pan. Serves 6 to 8.

BEANS AND ROAST PORK

1 pound dried white beans	1 clove garlic
1 teaspoon herb-bouquet blend	5-pound loin of pork
	Salt and pepper

Cover washed beans with 6 cups water, bring to boil and boil 2 minutes. Cover and let stand 1 hour; then cook with herbs and garlic until tender. Drain; remove garlic. Put meat on rack in roasting pan. Surround with beans. Season. Roast in moderate oven (325°F.) 3 hours, or until meat is done. Stir beans occasionally, adding water if necessary. Slice pork; serve with beans. Serves 6 to 8.

FLORENTINE PORK COOKED IN MILK

4-pound loin of pork, boned
Salt and pepper
1 tablespoon dried
  rosemary, crumbled
2 tablespoons butter
1 quart milk
1 can (4 ounces) mushrooms,
  undrained

Trim excess fat from meat. Rub with salt, pepper and rosemary. Brown on all sides in butter; add milk. Cover tightly and simmer over low heat 2 to 2½ hours. (Gravy will be thick and creamy and golden brown.) At serving time, place pork on hot serving platter and slice. Strain liquid, if desired, and add mushrooms. Thicken with flour-and-water paste, if desired. Pour gravy over sliced pork. Makes 6 to 8 servings.

Note Use ¼ pound fresh mushrooms, sliced and sautéed in butter, if desired.

FRENCH COUNTRY-STYLE PORK CHOPS

4 medium carrots
2 small white turnips
2 stalks celery
4 leeks, white part only,
  or 8 green onions, white
  part only
4 small white onions,
  chopped
1 can (28 ounces) tomatoes
⅛ teaspoon marjoram
1 bay leaf
¼ cup chopped parsley
¾ teaspoon salt
½ teaspoon pepper
⅓ cup consomme
1½ to 2 pounds rib or
  shoulder pork chops,
  trimmed of excess fat

Cut first 4 ingredients into 1½"-long julienne strips. Combine with next 8 ingredients in large kettle; bring to a boil. Simmer, covered, 5 minutes. Put pork chops on top of vegetables. Cover and simmer about 1 hour, or until thoroughly done. Arrange vegetables in center of serving dish and surround with pork chops. Makes 4 servings.

PORK-CHOP AND SWEET-POTATO SKILLET

Chops are topped with sweet potatoes, onion, green pepper, tomatoes.

4 pork chops
1 tablespoon fat
Salt and pepper
¼ teaspoon each thyme and marjoram

1 onion, sliced
4 sweet potatoes, peeled and sliced
1 green pepper, cut in rings
1 can (19 ounces) tomatoes

Brown chops on both sides in fat in skillet. Season with salt, pepper and herbs. Top with onion, potatoes and pepper; add tomatoes. Cover; cook slowly 45 minutes. Makes 4 servings.

SWEET AND SOUR SPARERIBS

3 pounds spareribs, cut in 1½"-wide pieces
3 tablespoons flour
1 cup diced celery
1 cup chopped green pepper
1 medium onion, chopped

½ cup maple syrup or substitute
1 can (1 pound) pineapple chunks with syrup
¼ cup vinegar
⅓ cup soy sauce
Salt and pepper to taste

Roast spareribs in hot oven (400°F.) 30 minutes, or until golden brown, stirring occasionally. Remove ribs from roasting pan and drain off all but ¼ cup drippings. Blend in flour, add remaining ingredients and mix well. Put ribs in sauce and bake in moderate oven (375°F.) 1½ hours, or until tender, basting often. Remove ribs to a hot serving dish and top with sauce. Thicken sauce if necessary with 1 tablespoon cornstarch blended with a little water. Serves 4.

BAKED HAM SLICE WITH APPLE RINGS

1½-pound center-cut fully-cooked ham slice, about 1" thick
¾ cup packed brown sugar

½ teaspoon each ground cloves and cinnamon
3 medium tart apples
½ cup pineapple juice

Gash fat in ham slice to prevent curling. Mix brown sugar and spices and rub one fourth of mixture into one side of ham. Put sugar side down in shallow baking dish. Peel and core apples and cut in ½" slices. Arrange around ham. Sprinkle apples and ham with remaining sugar mixture. Heat juice to boiling and pour over all. Bake, uncovered, in moderate oven (350°F.) about 45 minutes. Remove ham and apples to hot platter and pour liquid over all. Makes 4 servings.

HAM IN CIDER

½ bone-in, cook-before-
eating smoked ham
(about 6 pounds)
Cider (about 2 to 3 quarts)
2 large carrots, scraped
and sliced
1 bay leaf

3 medium onions, peeled
and sliced
3 stalks celery, diced
Few sprigs of parsley
12 whole cloves
6 whole black peppercorns

Put ham in kettle; add enough cider to cover. Add remaining ingredients. Bring to boil, cover and simmer 2 hours, or until tender. Serve hot. Or cool in the broth, then chill. Makes 8 servings.

ALSATIAN CHOUCROUTE

4 strips bacon, diced
2 onions, chopped
2 pounds fresh or 1 can
(29 ounces) sauerkraut,
drained
1 large carrot, peeled and
diced
1 large potato, peeled and
grated
3 apples, peeled and diced

1 pound knackwurst or
kielbasa
1 slice ham, cut in 1" squares
2 fresh pork hocks
10 dried juniper berries
5 peppercorns
1 cup meat stock
1 cup dry white wine
Boiled potatoes

Sauté bacon and onion until limp but not brown. In large heavy casserole, mix sauerkraut with all vegetables, apple, bacon and bacon fat. Cut 1 knackwurst in ½" slices and add with ham and hocks to casserole.

Crush berries; tie with peppercorns in cheesecloth and add to casserole. Pour stock and wine over the mixture; cover tightly and bake in moderate oven (350°F.) for 2 to 2½ hours. Check for dryness the last half hour, adding more stock if needed. Put rest of knackwurst, cut in half, on top. Cover and finish cooking. Remove spices in cloth. Serve with boiled potatoes. Makes 6 to 8 servings.

SKILLET FRANKS WITH BEANS

6 frankfurters, sliced
2 teaspoons instant minced onion
¼ teaspoon instant minced garlic (optional)
¼ teaspoon crushed dried oregano leaves

1 tablespoon butter or margarine
1 can (28 ounces) New England-style baked beans
1 medium tomato, cut in thin wedges

Sauté first 4 ingredients in butter until frankfurter slices are lightly browned. Add beans and heat well. Add tomato wedges and heat gently. Makes 4 servings.

BAKED SAUSAGE, CABBAGE AND APPLES

1 pound sausage meat
3 tablespoons vinegar
1 teaspoon instant minced onion
2 tablespoons brown sugar
Salt and pepper

1 small cabbage, finely shredded (about 4 cups)
4 cups thinly sliced peeled tart apples
Nutmeg

Shape sausage meat in 8 flat patties. Brown on both sides in skillet, cooking until almost done. Remove sausage from skillet and add next 3 ingredients to fat. (If amount of fat seems excessive, pour off some.) Season with salt and pepper. Alternate layers of cabbage and apples in 3-quart casserole, seasoning each layer with salt, pepper and nutmeg. Arrange sausage patties on top and pour vinegar mixture over meat. Cover and bake in moderate oven (375°F.) about 45 minutes. Serves 4.

POLENTA CON SALSICCE

(Italian Cornmeal Mush with Sausages)

1 pound Italian sausage, sweet or hot	1 tablespoon parsley, chopped
1 tablespoon olive oil	¼ teaspoon oregano
1 large onion, chopped	½ teaspoon basil
2 cloves garlic, minced	Cayenne and salt
1 can (35 ounces) Italian tomatoes	1 cup cornmeal, yellow or white
1 can (6 ounces) tomato paste	¼ cup butter
1 teaspoon sugar	Grated Parmesan cheese

Cut sausage in ½" slices and brown slowly in oil with onion and garlic until vegetables are limp. Add next 7 ingredients with ½ teaspoon salt and simmer 1 to 1½ hours. Combine cornmeal, 3 cups water and 1 teaspoon salt in double boiler. Let simmer 1 hour after thickening. Cool slightly and beat in butter and ½ cup grated Parmesan. Spread in 8" x 8" x 2" cake pan. Chill until firm, overnight if possible. Cut in 2" squares; put on large flat shallow baking dish. Top with sauce; put in hot oven (400°F.) 20 minutes. Remove and top with more cheese. Broil until cheese melts. Makes 6 to 8 servings.

GROUND MEAT

HOW TO BUY GROUND MEAT

Grinding meats is a method of tenderizing them and is also a good way for butchers to use up the trimmings from larger cuts. Ground meat may be beef (hamburger), veal, lamb, pork, or meat-loaf mixture, which contains beef, pork and veal.

• Beef, of course, is the most popular kind of ground meat, is available in several types and is usually ground twice. It can be ground to order. **Regular ground beef,** the lowest in price, is the highest in fat content. **Ground chuck,** containing from 10 to 20 percent fat, is medium priced. **Ground round,** with less than 10 percent fat, is usually more expensive.

• Veal flank, breast, shank, neck, shoulder or round is usually ground with added meat fat and often with other meats.

• Lamb neck, shoulder, flank, breast or shank may be ground for use in loaves, patties and casseroles.

• Ground pork is not available prepackaged but can be ground to order. It is often used in combination with beef to add extra flavor as in meat loaves and meatballs. Always cook it well done.

• Meat-loaf mixture, usually ground beef, veal and pork, is available prepackaged. Always be sure that it is cooked well done.

STORAGE OF GROUND MEAT

Ground meat should be wrapped loosely in waxed paper and stored in the coldest part of the refrigerator. Use within 24 hours. Beef keeps a little longer than the other meats.

BACON NUTBURGERS

6 slices bacon	6 tablespoons chopped nuts
1½ pounds ground chuck	3 tablespoons chopped
1½ teaspoons salt	parsley
⅛ teaspoon pepper	2 tablespoons grated onion

Cook bacon until crisp; drain. Mix beef, salt and pepper; divide in 12 equal portions and roll with rolling pin between 2 sheets of waxed paper to form thin patties about 5″ in diameter. Mix last 3 ingredients and spread on 6 patties. Top each with a bacon slice. Cover with remaining 6 patties and crimp edges with fork. Broil to desired doneness, turning once. Makes 6 servings.

BURGERS IN PEPPER RINGS

1 pound ground chuck	6 green-pepper rings, about
¾ cup soft bread crumbs	½" thick
1 teaspoon salt	1 tablespoon fat
⅛ teaspoon pepper	Bottled barbecue sauce
¼ cup milk	6 split sandwich rolls, heated

Mix first 5 ingredients and shape in 6 patties. Press the mixture into pepper rings, having meat cover cut edge of pepper on both sides. Brown patties on both sides in hot fat in skillet. Baste generously with sauce. Cook to desired doneness and serve in rolls. Makes 6 servings.

DILL BURGERS

Add ½ teaspoon crushed dillseed and ¼ cup chopped olives or sweet pickles to 1 pound ground beef. Season to taste and shape in patties; cook to desired doneness. Serves 3.

SESAME BURGERS

Toast ¼ cup sesame seed in moderate oven (350°F.) 10 to 15 minutes. Add to 1 pound ground beef; season, shape in patties and broil or panfry to desired doneness. Serves 3.

HAMBURGER TOPPINGS

Spread on broiled, grilled or panfried hamburgers just before serving.

Cranberry-Celery Sauce Mix 1 cup cranberry sauce, ¼ cup sliced celery, 1 teaspoon lemon juice and 1 teaspoon minced onion.

Savory Butter Cream ½ cup butter. Stir in 2 tablespoons each chopped parsley and green-onion tops.

Blue-cheese Topping Mix 2 ounces blue cheese and ½ teaspoon steak sauce.

Steak-sauce Butter Mix ¼ cup soft butter and 2 tablespoons steak sauce.

PIZZA MEAT LOAF

1 pound ground beef	Garlic salt
1 teaspoon salt	Onion salt
¼ teaspoon pepper	¼ teaspoon basil
1 cup well-drained canned tomatoes	Few sprigs of parsley, chopped
½ cup shredded sharp Cheddar cheese	1 can (2 ounces) flat anchovy fillets

Mix first 3 ingredients lightly but thoroughly and press into an 8″ piepan, making a shell. Bake in hot oven (400°F.) 10 minutes. Remove from oven and pour off fat and liquid. Spread with tomatoes and cover with cheese. Sprinkle lightly with garlic and onion salts, the basil and parsley. Arrange anchovies spoke-fashion on top. Return to oven and bake 15 minutes longer. Cut in wedges. Serves 4.

BEEF OATMEAL LOAF

2 pounds ground beef
2½ teaspoons salt
¼ teaspoon each pepper
  and nutmeg

1 onion, minced
1 cup quick-cooking rolled
  oats
1 can (19 ounces) tomatoes

Mix first 5 ingredients. Force tomatoes through coarse sieve; combine with meat mixture. Shape in large flat loaf or 2 small loaves in baking pan; crisscross top surface with a knife. Bake in moderate oven (350°F.) 1½ hours for large loaf, 1 hour for small loaves. Serves 8 to 10.

BEEF-CARROT-OLIVE LOAF

2 pounds ground beef
  chuck
1½ cups cornflakes
½ cup chopped parsley
½ cup shredded raw carrot
1 can (4½ ounces) chopped
  ripe olives
1 medium onion, chopped
2 cloves garlic, minced

2 tablespoons butter or
  margarine
2 teaspoons salt
½ teaspoon pepper
½ teaspoon each sage and
  oregano
1½ cups milk
1 egg

Mix first 5 ingredients. Add onion and garlic, browned in butter, and remaining ingredients. Mix well and shape in a loaf in a baking pan. Bake in moderate oven (350°F.) about 1 hour. Makes 8 servings.

SWEDISH MEATBALLS

1 onion, minced
Butter
1 pound ground lean beef
½ pound each ground lean
  pork and veal
1 cup dry stale-bread
  crumbs
1 cup milk
2 eggs, beaten
Dash of nutmeg

1 teaspoon salt
⅛ teaspoon pepper
3 tablespoons flour
2 cups meat stock or
  consomme
Pinch of grated lemon rind
1 cup dairy sour cream
Chopped dill or parsley
Cooked noodles

Sauté onion in 1 tablespoon butter; add to next 8 ingredients, mixing with hands to get even texture. Roll in small balls. Brown in 2 tablespoons butter. Remove meatballs. To pan juices, add flour and stock to make gravy. Stir until hot. Check seasoning and add lemon rind. (Gravy should not be too thick at this point.) Return meatballs to gravy and simmer over very low heat 1 hour. Remove meatballs to serving dish with slotted spoon. Stir sour cream into gravy and heat. Pour over meat; add dill. Serve with noodles. Makes 6 to 8 servings.

DOLMATHES

(Stuffed Grape Leaves)

1 pound ground lean beef	2 tablespoons olive oil
3 eggs	Salt and pepper
1 medium onion, chopped	Grape or cabbage leaves
½ cup uncooked rice	2 cans condensed beef
¼ cup chopped parsley	bouillon, heated
1 teaspoon chopped fresh	Juice of 1 lemon
mint leaves (or ½ teaspoon	
dried)	

Mix beef, 1 egg, beaten, next 5 ingredients and ¼ cup water. Season. Soak fresh grape or cabbage leaves in hot water 5 minutes to soften. (Remove core of cabbage and soak whole head so that leaves can be peeled off without breaking.) Rinse canned grape leaves in warm water. Place a spoonful of meat mixture on a leaf (shiny side is down) and roll, folding ends to seal in mixture. Place folded side down in skillet, making 2 layers if necessary. Add beef bouillon and 1½ cups water. Cover and simmer 45 minutes. Remove to hot platter. For sauce, add lemon juice to remaining eggs, beaten. Slowly add some hot broth to eggs; continue to beat. Stir egg mixture into remaining broth. Remove from heat, cover and allow to stand 5 minutes to thicken. Pour over Dolmathes. Makes 6 servings.

HAMBURGER PIE

This recipe comes from Canada.

1 box pastry mix	1½ cups dry bread cubes
½ cup grated sharp Cheddar cheese	1 can condensed beef bouillon or consommé
½ teaspoon paprika	½ teaspoon salt
Dash of cayenne	½ teaspoon pepper
1½ pounds ground beef chuck	¼ teaspoon each thyme and marjoram
1 small onion, minced	2 teaspoons Worcestershire

Prepare pastry mix as directed on the label, adding cheese, paprika and cayenne before adding the liquid. Roll half of pastry on lightly floured board and fit in 9″ piepan. Cook beef and onion in skillet until meat loses its red color, breaking up meat with fork. Mix bread cubes and bouillon and let stand a few minutes. Add beef mixture and remaining ingredients. Mix well and pour into pie shell. Roll remaining pastry and put over top, crimping edges. Bake in moderate oven (375°F.) about 45 minutes. Serve warm or cold. Makes 6 servings.

EASY CHILI CON CARNE WITH BEANS

1 pound ground beef
1 large onion, chopped
2 cloves garlic, crushed
½ teaspoon salt
2 to 3 teaspoons chili
    powder
Dash of pepper

1 tablespoon shortening
1 can condensed tomato
    soup
2 cans (1 pound each)
    kidney beans, undrained
1 teaspoon vinegar

Brown first 6 ingredients lightly in the shortening. Add remaining ingredients and ½ cup water. Bring to boil, cover and cook over low heat, stirring occasionally, about 30 minutes. Makes 4 servings.

MUSAKA, YUGOSLAV STYLE

3 medium eggplants
Salt
Flour
7 eggs
⅔ cup vegetable oil
3 large onions, minced
½ cup butter or margarine
½ pound each ground lean
    pork and beef

1 pound ground lamb
¼ cup fine dry bread crumbs
½ teaspoon pepper
1 clove garlic, minced
2 cups milk
⅛ teaspoon nutmeg
3 egg yolks, beaten
Dairy sour cream (optional)

Peel eggplants and cut in ¼″ lengthwise slices. Sprinkle generously with salt and let stand 15 minutes. Dust with flour. Then dip in 5 eggs, beaten, and brown quickly on both sides in hot oil. Set aside. In skillet cook onion in ¼ cup butter until golden. Mix meats with next three ingredients, ½ teaspoon salt and 2 eggs. Add to onion. Cook and stir until meat is crumbled and lightly browned. In saucepan melt ¼ cup butter and blend in 6 tablespoons flour. Gradually add milk and cook, stirring, until smooth and thickened. Stir in ½ teaspoon salt and the nutmeg. Stir a little of the hot sauce into the egg yolks; stir mixture into sauce. Line a 3½- to 4-quart shallow baking dish or roasting pan with a layer of eggplant. Top with a layer of meat mixture. Repeat layers until all eggplant and meat are used, ending with eggplant. Pour sauce over top. Bake in moderate oven (375°F.) 1 hour. Cut in squares. Serve with sour cream if desired. Makes 10 servings.

CHILI MEATBALLS

1 pound meat-loaf mixture
¼ cup white cornmeal
1 clove garlic, crushed or minced
1 small onion, g.ated
1 teaspoon ground coriander
1 teaspoon salt
¼ teaspoon pepper
Sauce

Mix lightly all ingredients, except Sauce. Shape in balls about ¾" in diameter. Drop into boiling Sauce, cover and simmer 10 to 15 minutes. Makes 4 servings.

Sauce Melt 1 tablespoon butter in saucepan; add 1 small onion, chopped and 1 clove garlic, crushed and minced. Cook slowly until lightly browned. Add 1 tablespoon chili powder and 1 can (1 pint 2 ounces) tomato juice; simmer 10 minutes. Season with salt and pepper.

STUFFED GREEN PEPPERS

4 large green peppers
1½ cups ground cooked
   meat
¼ cup uncooked rice
¼ cup minced onion
1½ teaspoons salt

¼ teaspoon pepper
1 can (8 ounces) tomato
   sauce
Dash of cayenne
2 basil leaves, or pinch of
   dried basil

Cut off tops of peppers and remove seeds. Mix next 5 ingredients. Stuff peppers three fourths full. Stand up in deep heavy skillet with tight-fitting lid. Pour remaining ingredients mixed with 1 cup water over peppers. Cover and cook very slowly 40 minutes. If necessary, add a little more water. Makes 4 servings.

POULTRY

HOW TO BUY POULTRY

Today most poultry comes from the market in ready-to-cook form. Whole birds are sold eviscerated with edible giblets wrapped separately in the body cavity. Most markets sell both chilled freshly-killed and frozen birds. There is also a choice, in the case of chicken and turkey, of whole or cut-up birds and parts (breasts, thighs, wings, necks and backs) and frozen boneless chicken and turkey rolls. Chicken livers and giblets are also sold separately.

Amounts to buy

Allow ½ to ¾ pound per person for ready-to-cook chicken; ¾ to 1 pound for turkey, guinea hen and capon; 1 to 1½ pounds for duck and geese.

POULTRY STORAGE

If **chilled fresh ready-to-cook,** remove wrapper. Remove giblets and neck from cavity. Wrap bird loosely in waxed paper, foil or plastic wrap and store in coldest part of refrigerator. Use within 24 hours. If **quick-frozen ready-to-cook,** put bird in freezer as quickly as possible. Keep frozen stored at 0°F., or less, until ready to thaw for cooking. Completely thaw bird before cooking, following label directions. Once thawed, remove giblets and neck and cook bird at once. **To store leftover roast bird,** remove stuffing while bird is still warm and refrigerate separately. It is not necessary for poultry to cool at room temperature longer than 15 to 20 minutes before refrigerating.

Caution

Do not stuff bird with warm stuffing and store in refrigerator until ready to roast. If stuffing must be made ahead, refrigerate separately and stuff bird just before roasting.

ROAST CHICKEN WITH SAUSAGE-NUT STUFFING

1 roasting chicken (3 to 4
   pounds)
1 lemon
¼ cup sausage meat
¼ cup butter or margarine
3 tablespoons minced onion
½ teaspoon paprika
¾ teaspoon salt
¼ cup chopped celery
¼ cup chopped parsley

3½ cups soft stale-bread
   crumbs
⅓ cup chopped pecans
Milk
1 tablespoon chicken or
   sausage fat
Celery leaves and rosemary
½ cup cream
2 tablespoons brown sugar

Wash and dry chicken. Rub skin with cut lemon. Cook sausage until golden brown, breaking up with fork. Add butter and 2 tablespoons of the onion. Cook 2 or 3 minutes. Remove from heat and add next 6 ingredients. Mix well with enough milk to moisten. Stuff body and neck cavities of chicken lightly and truss. Rub with fat; then sprinkle with celery leaves, rosemary and remaining 1 tablespoon onion. Wrap loosely in foil and put on rack in open shallow pan. Roast in slow oven (325°F.) 1½ hours. Pull foil away from chicken. Brush with mixture of cream and brown sugar. Continue roasting and basting 1 hour, or until chicken is tender and well browned. Serves 4 to 6.

CHICKEN WITH GINGER-CREAM SAUCE

1 frying chicken (about
   2½ pounds), cut up
¼ cup flour
½ teaspoon salt
⅛ teaspoon pepper
1 teaspoon ginger

3 tablespoons butter
1 chicken bouillon cube
½ cup cream
Hot cooked green lima
   beans

Roll chicken in mixture of flour, salt, pepper and ginger. Brown in butter. Stir in remaining flour mixture. Add bouillon cube dissolve in ¾ cup boiling water and bring to boil. Cover and simmer 45 minutes, or until tender. Stir in cream and heat. Serve with lima beans. Makes 4 servings.

CHICKEN, JAMAICA STYLE

1 roasting chicken (about
   4 pounds)
2 tablespoons butter or
   margarine
1½ cups chicken broth
¾ cup sliced celery
1 medium onion, chopped
½ teaspoon garlic salt

2 dried red peppers,
   crushed
1 tablespoon vinegar
¼ teaspoon allspice
½ cup sliced green olives
1 medium green pepper,
   sliced
2 tablespoons cornstarch
Salt and pepper

Brown chicken on all sides in butter in heavy kettle. Put chicken on rack in kettle. Add next 7 ingredients, cover and simmer 1½ hours, or until chicken is tender. Add olives and green pepper and cook 10 minutes longer. Remove chicken and thicken liquid with corn-starch blended with a little cold water. Pour over chicken. Season. Serves 4.

SOUTHERN FRIED CHICKEN WITH CREAM GRAVY

1 frying chicken (about 2½ pounds), cut up	Butter
All-purpose flour	Solid vegetable shortening
1½ teaspoons salt	2 cups light cream
¾ teaspoon pepper	Hot corn bread

Shake moist pieces of chicken, a few at a time, in a paper bag with ½ cup flour, the salt and the pepper until thoroughly coated. Melt equal amounts of butter and shortening to ½″ depth in large, heavy, covered skillet. Put in chicken; cover and brown quickly in hot fat on all sides. Reduce heat and continue frying slowly 25 minutes, turning once or twice. Remove cover during last 10 minutes cooking. Remove chicken. Drain off all but 2 tablespoons fat from pan; stir in 2 tablespoons flour. Add cream gradually, stirring constantly. Season and cook until thickened. Serve with gravy and corn bread. Makes 4 servings.

CHICKEN KIEV

From Russia, thin pieces of chicken wrapped around butter.

1½ sticks butter (6 ounces)	3 eggs
6 chicken breasts	Fat for deep frying
Fine dry bread crumbs	

Halve butter lengthwise; cut in twelve 2″ pieces. Chill until very firm. Cut chicken breasts in half; remove bones. On wet board, pound chicken into thin cutlets. Put a piece of butter in center of each. Roll chicken around butter; fold securely so butter cannot escape during cooking. Secure with toothpicks. Roll in bread crumbs; dip in eggs beaten with 2 tablespoons cold water; roll again in crumbs. Fry in hot deep fat (375°F. on frying thermometer) 3 to 5 minutes. Drain and put on cookie sheet in hot oven (425°F.) 5 minutes. Makes 6 servings.

CHICKEN, HAWAIIAN STYLE

A luscious party dish, rich with herbs and spices.

1 frying chicken (about 2½ pounds), cut up
¼ cup soy sauce
½ cup dry white wine
Juice of 1 lime
1 clove garlic, crushed
1 teaspoon curry powder
1 teaspoon minced fresh ginger or ground ginger to taste
¼ teaspoon each thyme, oregano and pepper
2 medium onions, thinly sliced
5 tablespoons butter or margarine
Seasoned flour
1½ cups uncooked rice
4 canned pineapple slices, halved
½ cup toasted slivered almonds
8 soft prunes, pitted and cut up
1 pimiento, minced

Wash and dry chicken pieces. Mix soy sauce, ¼ cup wine and next 5 ingredients. Pour over chicken and marinate several hours, turning occasionally. Cook onions in 4 tablespoons butter until golden. Remove onions. Remove chicken from marinade, dry and dredge with flour. Brown in drippings in skillet. Add onions and marinade, cover and cook 45 minutes, uncovering pan last 15 minutes. Meanwhile, cook and drain rice and keep hot. Brown pineapple slices in 1 tablespoon butter. To serve, mix rice, almonds, prunes and pimiento and heap on large serving platter. Arrange chicken and pineapple slices around edge. Add ¼ cup wine to drippings. Heat well and serve as sauce. Makes 4 servings.

ARROZ CON POLLO

(Spanish Chicken with Rice)

From Spain, chicken, onion, pepper, tomatoes and rice, cooked together.

1 frying chicken (about 2½ pounds), cut up	¼ teaspoon pepper
Salt	Pinch of saffron
3 tablespoons olive oil	½ teaspoon paprika
1 large onion, chopped	2 whole cloves
1 clove garlic, minced	1 bay leaf
1 medium green pepper, chopped	1¼ cups uncooked long-grain rice
1 can (19 ounces) tomatoes	1 cup cooked peas
⅓ cup sherry	1 pimiento, cut up

Season chicken with salt. Brown in oil. Add onion, garlic and green pepper; brown about 5 minutes. Add next 7 ingredients and 1 cup water. Cover; simmer 15 minutes. Add rice, bring to boil and stir. Cover; simmer about 30 minutes. Garnish with peas and pimiento. Serves 4 to 6.

CHICKEN BREASTS GRUYÈRE

2 whole chicken breasts
Salt and pepper
3 tablespoons butter or
 margarine
4 large mushrooms, chopped

2 tablespoons flour
1¼ cups milk
¼ pound natural Gruyère
 cheese, finely shredded
 (about 1 cup)

Split, skin and bone breasts. Sprinkle with salt and pepper. In skillet, sauté chicken, turning, in 1 tablespoon melted butter 10 minutes, or until done. Remove to broiler-proof platter. Sauté mushrooms in same skillet and spoon over chicken. Melt remaining 2 tablespoons butter in skillet and stir in flour. Slowly stir in milk and simmer about 5 minutes. Stir in cheese until melted. Add additional salt to taste. Spoon over chicken (sauce will be very thick). Broil until browned. Makes 4 servings.

TURKEY TETRAZZINI

¾ pound mushrooms, sliced
1 small green pepper,
 slivered
¼ cup butter or margarine
3 tablespoons flour
2 teaspoons salt
¼ teaspoon pepper
2½ cups light cream

4 cups diced cooked turkey
2 pimientos, chopped
2 tablespoons sherry
6 ounces fine spaghetti,
 cooked
2 egg yolks, beaten
Grated Parmesan cheese

Cook mushrooms and green pepper in the butter 5 minutes. Blend in flour and seasonings. Add cream and cook, stirring, until thickened. Add next 3 ingredients and heat. Divide spaghetti into 6 broiler-proof individual baking dishes or put in shallow baking dish. Add small amount of turkey mixture to egg yolks, then return, stirring, to turkey mixture. Pour over spaghetti and sprinkle with cheese. Bake in slow oven (300°F.) about 45 minutes. Put under broiler to brown lightly. Makes 6 servings.

TURKEY PIE WITH SAGE PASTRY

½ cup butter
½ cup all-purpose flour
1¼ teaspoons salt
¼ teaspoon ground sage
⅛ teaspoon pepper
⅛ teaspoon mace

1 teaspoon lemon juice
1½ cups turkey or chicken broth
1 cup milk
3 cups diced cooked turkey
Sage pastry

Melt butter; blend in flour and seasonings. Add lemon juice, stock and milk. Cook, stirring, until thickened. Add turkey and heat. Pour into shallow 1½-quart casserole. Roll Sage Pastry to fit top of casserole. Set in place, trim and flute edges. Cut 2 or 3 gashes in top to allow steam to escape. Bake in hot oven (425°F.) about 20 minutes. Makes 6 servings.

Sage Pastry Mix ½ cup all-purpose flour, ½ cup cornmeal, ½ teaspoon each salt and ground sage. Cut in ⅓ cup butter or margarine. Add 3 tablespoons water; mix lightly with fork.

LEMON-GLAZED DUCK

1 duckling (4 to 5 pounds)
Salt and pepper
Grated rind and juice of
 1 lemon

½ cup honey
1 lemon, peeled and thinly
 sliced
Watercress or parsley

Wash duckling and dry on absorbent paper. Sprinkle inside and out with salt and pepper. Truss bird and place on rack in shallow roasting pan. If desired, prick skin all over to allow fat to drain out. Roast in slow oven (325°F.) about 3 hours. Pour off fat during roasting. Mix lemon rind and juice and honey. During last hour of roasting, brush frequently with the mixture. Remove to serving platter and garnish with sliced lemon and watercress. Makes 3 to 4 servings.

BROILED CORNISH HENS

2 Rock Cornish hens, split
Salt and white pepper

1 teaspoon crushed dried
 marjoram or thyme leaves
Melted butter or margarine

Rub hens with salt, pepper and marjoram; let stand about 1 hour. Put, skin side down, in preheated broiler. Brush with melted butter and broil about 5″ from unit 12 to 15 minutes. Turn and brush with butter, broil 12 to 15 minutes, or until tender and well browned. Makes 4 servings.

ROAST GOOSE WITH SAVORY FRUIT STUFFING

1 junior goose (about 12 pounds)	1½ cups cranberries
1 lemon	1½ cups each finely diced celery and apple
Salt and pepper	½ teaspoon salt
1½ cups chopped pitted prunes	

Remove excess fat and rub goose inside and out with cut lemon. Sprinkle with salt and pepper. Mix remaining ingredients and lightly stuff cavity of goose. Skewer or sew opening, truss bird and put breast down on rack in shallow roasting pan. Roast in slow oven (325°F.) 4½ hours, or until drumstick meat feels very soft. Prick skin occasionally and pour off fat as it accumulates in pan. After about 3 hours of roasting, turn goose over and finish roasting. Makes 8 to 10 servings.

Note Seasoned with apple and onion, goose fat makes an excellent fat for frying potatoes, or shortening for biscuits or other hot breads. Rinse fat and cut in small pieces. Put in heavy saucepan and cover with cold water. Add 1 apple, cut in wedges, and 1 small onion. Cook, uncovered, over low heat until all water is evaporated. Strain into container, cool and chill.

FISH, SHELLFISH

HOW TO BUY FISH AND SHELLFISH

Although canned, frozen and dried fish and shellfish are available everywhere all through the year, fresh fish is another story. The kind you can buy in one area may not be in another. Seasonal factors, weather and yearly fluctuations affect the catch and determine the kind and amount of fish that comes to our markets. And since fresh fish is highly perishable, market storage is often a problem. So it's a good idea to buy with special care. Fresh fish should smell fresh and have firm elastic flesh and bulging eyes. Shells of oysters and clams should be tightly closed. Uncooked lobsters or crabs should be alive when purchased. Fresh scallops are at their best from November to April; oysters, September through

April. Fresh Northern lobsters are most plentiful in summer.

Amounts of fish to buy

Allow about 1½ pounds fresh or frozen fillets for 4 servings, about 2 pounds steaks and about 3 pounds whole fish.

> 1 dozen live clams or oysters = 2 servings
> 1 pint shucked clams = 3 servings
> 1 dozen live crabs = 4 servings
> 1 pound crab or lobster meat = 6 servings
> 1 pound live lobster = 1 serving
> 1 pint shucked oysters = 3 servings
> 1 pound scallops = 3 servings
> 1 pound shelled shrimps = 3 servings
> 1 pound lobster tails = 2 servings

FISH AND SHELLFISH STORAGE

All fresh fish and shellfish should be cooked as soon as possible after buying. If frozen fish has thawed, do not attempt to refreeze it, but cook it promptly.

Equivalents

6½-ounce can crab meat = ¾ cup meat
6½-ounce can lobster — 1 cup meat
6-ounce frozen lobster tail = ½ cup diced meat
4½-ounce can shrimps = 22 to 28 shrimps

CANNED-SALMON TIPS

Salmon color varies from deep red to light pink or almost white. The deep-red varieties are more oily and more expensive. The less expensive types are just as nutritious and can be used in any recipe where color is not important, such as sandwiches, casseroles and loaves. Where possible, use the salmon liquid, skin and the soft bones (which may be mashed) because they contain nutrients.

TROUT WITH ANCHOVY SAUCE

4 trout
Seasoned flour
Olive oil
3 tablespoons butter
4 anchovy fillets, cut fine
½ cup white wine

1 teaspoon chopped fresh
   or dried mint
1 tablespoon chopped
   parsley
Juice of 1 lemon

Roll fish in seasoned flour. Heat enough olive oil to cover bottom of skillet. Panfry fish about 5 minutes on each side. Meanwhile, melt butter, add anchovy fillets and heat 5 minutes. Add next 3 ingredients, simmer 3 minutes; add lemon juice. Put fish on hot platter and pour sauce over all. Makes 4 servings.

SOLE IN VERMOUTH

1 cup dry vermouth
1½ pounds sole fillets
4 egg yolks

⅔ cup butter or margarine
1 tablespoon heavy cream
Salt and pepper

Heat vermouth in skillet. Wrap fish loosely in cheese-cloth and poach in the vermouth about 10 minutes. Put fish on broilerproof platter. Boil vermouth to reduce to about ⅔ cup. Put in top of double boiler with next 3 ingredients. Cook over hot, not boiling, water, stirring until mixture just begins to thicken. Season, pour over fish and brown very quickly under broiler. Serves 4 to 6.

LEMON BAKED FISH

1 pound fish fillets
Juice of 1 lemon
1 teaspoon salt
1½ teaspoons dried dill
½ teaspoon paprika

1 tablespoon butter or
  margarine
1 lemon, peeled and thinly
  sliced
1 tablespoon parsley flakes

Place fish in greased baking dish and sprinkle with lemon juice and seasonings. Dot with butter. Arrange lemon slices on fish. Bake in slow oven (325°F.) 20 minutes, or until fish flakes easily with fork. Sprinkle with parsley flakes. Makes 4 servings.

BAKED WHOLE FISH

Stuff whole red snapper, bluefish or haddock lightly with well-seasoned bread stuffing. Cut 3 or 4 gashes in skin and insert thin slices of salt pork or bacon. Put a pinch of thyme or marjoram, 1 minced onion, 3 tablespoons minced parsley and 2 tablespoons fat in baking pan. Put fish in pan; bake in moderate oven (350°F.) until fish flakes easily with a fork. Makes 4 to 6 servings.

BAKED SALMON WITH CAPER BUTTER

4 salmon steaks, 1″ to 1½″
  thick
⅓ cup lemon juice
½ cup butter

Salt and pepper
¼ cup chopped parsley
½ cup chopped capers

Rub salmon steaks with part of lemon juice, brush well with melted butter and sprinkle with salt and pepper. Arrange in baking dish and bake in hot oven (425°F.) about 20 minutes, basting several times with melted butter and lemon juice. Do not turn. Add parsley and capers and baste again. If additional liquid is needed, add a little dry vermouth or white wine. Makes 4 servings.

HOT SALMON MOUSSE

1 can (1 pound) red salmon	1 teaspoon onion juice
¾ teaspoon salt	3 egg whites
¼ teaspoon pepper	1 cup heavy cream
1 teaspoon Worcestershire	Mayonnaise

Drain salmon and remove skin. Whirl salmon in blender or force through food chopper, using fine blade. Add seasonings and mix well. Add egg whites one at a time, blending thoroughly after each addition. Add cream and mix well. Pour into well-oiled 1½-quart mold and set in pan of hot water. Bake in moderate oven (375°F.) 30 to 40 minutes, or until mixture is firm and inserted knife comes out clean. Unmold on hot platter and serve with mayonnaise. Makes 4 to 6 servings.

TUNA PATTIES, FINES HERBES

Serve on broiled or fried tomato slices.

Potatoes
2 cans (about 7 ounces each) tuna
3 eggs, beaten
Dash of pepper
2 tablespoons minced parsley
½ teaspoon thyme or marjoram
2 tablespoons minced chives
1 small clove garlic
½ teaspoon salt
Cracker crumbs
Olive oil, butter or other fat

Cook, drain and mash enough potatoes to make 3 cups. (Do not add milk.) Cool. Combine potatoes with next 6 ingredients. Add garlic peeled and mashed with salt. Form into patties, roll in crumbs and sauté in olive oil until browned on both sides. Makes 6 servings.

CHESAPEAKE CRAB CAKES

2 slices stale bread, crumbled
1 pound crab meat
2 egg yolks, beaten
1 teaspoon dry mustard
1 tablespoon butter, melted
1 tablespoon Worcestershire
Salt and pepper to taste
Fat for frying
Crackers
Tartar Sauce
Pickles

Mix all ingredients, except last 4, blend well and shape into 4 large or 8 smaller cakes. Chill at least 2 hours. Fry in 1″ fat in skillet, turning to brown. Drain on absorbent paper. If preferred, fry in deep fat. Serve with crackers, tartar sauce and pickles. Makes 4 servings.

Tartar Sauce Mix 1 cup mayonnaise, 1 teaspoon grated onion, 2 tablespoons chopped sweet pickle, and enough lemon juice to thin to desired consistency. For variety, add chopped parsley, chopped celery, capers, chopped olives, chili sauce or hot pepper sauce.

CREOLE CRAB CASSEROLE

⅔ cup uncooked rice
1 small onion, minced
1 small green pepper, chopped
2 tablespoons butter or margarine
1 can (1 pound) tomatoes
1 teaspoon seasoned salt
¼ teaspoon seasoned pepper
1 teaspoon sugar
½ teaspoon Worcestershire
1 bay leaf
6 whole black peppercorns
2 whole cloves
1 can (6-½ ounces) crab meat
Salt and pepper
¼ cup grated Parmesan cheese

Cook and drain rice. Cook onion and green pepper in butter 2 to 3 minutes. Add next 5 ingredients. Tie whole spices in small piece of cheesecloth and add. Simmer, uncovered, 10 minutes. Remove spice bag. Add crab meat, rice, and salt and pepper to taste. Put in 1½-quart casserole and sprinkle with cheese. Bake in moderate oven (375°F.) about 20 minutes. Makes 4 to 6 servings.

COQUILLES ST. JACQUES

(Scallops in Shells)

1½ pounds scallops	12 mushrooms chopped fine
Butter	Juice of 1 lemon
6 shallots or green onions, chopped	¼ teaspoon pepper
	3 tablespoons flour
Bouquet garni (parsley, celery, thyme, bay leaf)	4 egg yolks
	1 cup heavy cream
1½ cups dry white wine	Grated Parmesan cheese
Salt	Bread crumbs

Dry scallops on paper towels. Place in saucepan with 2 tablespoons butter, shallots and bouquet garni. Barely cover with white wine. Season with a little salt. Bring just to boil, reduce to a gentle simmer (the liquid should be just barely moving) and simmer 4 or 5 minutes, or until scallops are just tender. Drain and save broth for the sauce. Cut scallops in small pieces or slices. Sauté mushrooms a minute in 2 tablespoons butter. Add ⅓ cup water, the lemon juice, ½ teaspoon salt and the pepper. Simmer gently a few minutes. Drain and reserve liquid. Prepare a *beurre manié* with 3 tablespoons butter and the flour kneaded in small balls about the size of peas. Combine liquids from scallops and mushrooms in saucepan and heat. Stir in *beurre manié*. Cook and stir until sauce is thickened and smooth; cook 2 or 3 minutes. Add scallops and heat through. Beat egg yolks and mix with cream; add to sauce and cook gently, stirring, until smooth and thick. Do not let sauce boil. Add mushrooms and season. Spoon into individual ramekins or shells, sprinkle with Parmesan cheese and crumbs and lightly brown a minute under broiler. Makes 6 servings.

SCALLOPS EN BROCHETTE

Skewer alternately whole scallops, fresh mushrooms and squares of uncooked bacon. Grill over charcoal or in broiler about 10 minutes, turning often and brushing frequently with highly seasoned French dressing.

CIOPPINO

The versions of this stew are many. Traditional seasonings vary from area to area and the fish varies with the day's catch. In addition, individual cooks often change the ingredients to suit their own tastes. Some prefer white wine to red; others use sherry. Many like to add exotic tidbits such as octopus, squid or eel. Sometimes only shellfish are used. Soaked dried mushrooms are often included. This is the basic recipe. To prepare the fish and shellfish:

3 pounds sea bass, barracuda, halibut or a variety of any firm fish
1 large live Dungeness (hard-shell) crab or a live lobster
1 pound jumbo shrimps (or more)
1 pint clams, mussels or oysters, or all three

Cut the fish into good-size serving pieces. Crack the crab and remove the top shell but keep it for making stock. If you use lobster, cut the tail in pieces and reserve the body to make stock; if you use Eastern lobster, cut the tail in sections and crack the claws. Split the shrimp shells down the back and remove the black vein. Steam the mollusks (clams, mussels or oysters) in a small amount of water just until they open. Remove the top shells and save the juice. To prepare the sauce:

1½ cups chopped onion
1 cup chopped green
  pepper
¼ cup olive oil
3 cloves garlic thoroughly
  mashed with 1 teaspoon
  salt
1 can (29 ounces) tomatoes
Juice from the mollusks

2 cups red table wine
2 cups tomato juice
2 cups fish stock made from
  the crab shell or lobster
  body and fish trimmings
Herb bouquet (bay leaf,
  parsley, basil)
½ cup minced parsley

Sauté onion and green pepper in olive oil until just soft. Add rest of the ingredients, except parsley, and cook for 10 minutes. Remove herb bouquet and taste for seasoning. Arrange in layers all fish except the mollusks in large casserole or kettle with a cover. Pour sauce over fish. Simmer, covered, over low heat or in the oven for 20 to 30 minutes, or until the fish is just done. Add the mollusks for last 3 minutes. Serve in deep bowls, shells and all, and sprinkle liberally with minced parsley. This is finger food. Have plenty of big paper napkins on hand. Serve hot crusty sourdough bread and a robust red wine. For dessert, fruit and a variety of cheeses. Makes 4 servings.

OYSTERS ROCKEFELLER

2 dozen oysters with shells
1 tablespoon minced green
  onion
1 tablespoon chopped
  parsley
2 tablespoons butter or
  margarine

Salt, pepper and paprika
2 tablespoons minced bacon
2 tablespoons finely
  chopped cooked spinach
⅓ cup fine dry bread
  crumbs
Lemon wedges

Drain oysters on a paper towel. Wash shells and set on baking sheets with sides. Put an oyster in each shell. Mix onion, parsley and 1 tablespoon butter; dab on each oyster. Season with salt, pepper and paprika. Top with bacon, spinach and crumbs. Dot with 1 tablespoon butter. Bake in very hot oven (450°F.) 8 to 10 minutes. Serve with lemon. Serves 4.

SHRIMP CREOLE

1 medium onion, chopped
½ cup diced green pepper
2 tablespoons vegetable oil
1 clove garlic, minced
1 teaspoon salt
⅛ teaspoon pepper

1 can (1 pound) tomatoes
1 bay leaf
2 whole cloves
1½ pounds shrimp, cooked,
  shelled and cleaned

Cook onion and green pepper in the oil about 5 minutes. Add next 6 ingredients, bring to boil, cover and simmer 30 minutes. Remove cloves and bay leaf. Add shrimp and heat. Serve on rice. Makes 4 to 6 servings.

SHRIMP COOKED IN BEER

Prepare court bouillon for boiling shrimp, using 3 parts stale beer to 1 part water. Add 1 tablespoon salt for each quart liquid, a few whole black peppercorns, 1 or 2 bay leaves and a sprinkling of celery seed. Add shelled deveined shrimp and simmer, covered, 2 to 5 minutes, or until pink; drain. Use in recipes requiring cooked shrimp, or serve with favorite sauce.

CHEESE, EGGS

HOW TO BUY CHEESE

Versatile and varied, cheese can be served at any meal in any form—mixed into casseroles, melted into vegetable sauces, sprinkled on pasta or potatoes, or coupled with fruit for dessert. Cheese products are divided in four groups: **Natural cheese** (non-processed), made directly from milk curds or from whey; **process cheese,** composed of one or more natural cheeses; **process cheese food,** made with less cheese and more milk or water than process cheese; and **process cheese spread,** with an edible stabilizer added. Cheeses can also be classified as soft, semisoft, hard and very hard.

CHEESE STORAGE

Soft cheeses such as cottage cheese should be tightly covered and stored in the coldest part of the refrigerator.

Hard natural cheeses should be tightly wrapped in a double thickness of waxed paper, foil or plastic wrap and refrigerated. Cut edges can be buttered or coated with melted paraffin. Strong cheeses should be wrapped as above and put in a tightly covered container in the refrigerator. Mold on natural cheeses is not harmful and can be cut off. Process cheeses can be kept in their original wrapper or container in the refrigerator. Cheese spread in jars or crocks should be refrigerated after opening.

HOW TO BUY EGGS

Eggs are sold in cartons according to size, which is determined by weight per dozen as follows:

Jumbo	30 ounces or more
Extra large	27 ounces or more
Large	24 ounces or more
Medium	21 ounces or more
Small	18 ounces or more
Peewee	15 ounces or more

Buy the size that best suits your needs—smaller eggs may be an economy when used in cooking. Egg are graded according to freshness. Grade AA and Grade A eggs are top quality. They are best for poaching, frying and cooking in the shell. Grade B and Grade C eggs have thinner whites and rather flat yolks that may break easily. They are less expensive and are good to use for scrambling, baking, thickening sauces and to combine with other foods. Shell color is a matter of personal preference and has no effect on the taste or nutritional quality of the egg.

EGG STORAGE

Eggs should be stored, covered, in the refrigerator, away from strong-smelling foods and with small ends down.

To freeze eggs

WHOLE EGGS OR YOLKS To each 8-ounce cupful, add 1 tablespoon sugar or 1 teaspoon salt. Mix well with fork; freeze in freezer container. (Use sugared in cakes, puddings; salted in omelets, etc.) **WHITES** Freeze unbeaten.

Leftover yolks or whites

YOLKS They will keep 2 to 3 days in refrigerator if placed, covered with water, in jar with lid. **WHITES** They will keep up to 10 days in refrigerator if stored in covered jar.

COOKING CAUTION

Whether cooking eggs on top of range or in oven, always use low or moderate and even heat. If cooked at too high a temperature, eggs become tough. If adding hot liquids to beaten eggs, add just a little at a time, continuing to beat.

TO MEASURE EGGS

2 medium eggs = ⅓ cup
2 large eggs or 3 medium eggs = ½ cup
4 large eggs = 1 cup
6 large egg whites = 1 cup
12 large egg yolks = 1 cup

CHEESE FONDUE

Tradition says that if a lady drops bread into the fondue, the men at the table may kiss her; if a man drops bread into the cheese, he may kiss any girl he chooses.

1 clove garlic	Cognac, applejack or
2 cups dry white wine	vodka
1 pound Swiss cheese, finely	Pinch of nutmeg
cut	Dash of hot pepper sauce
1 teaspoon cornstarch	2 loaves Italian or French
3 tablespoons kirsch,	bread with hard crust

Rub an enameled metal casserole with garlic. Pour in wine and set over low heat. Heat until air bubbles rise to the surface and then add cheese by handfuls, stirring constantly with a wooden spoon or fork. Keep stirring until the cheese is melted. Add cornstarch dissolved in kirsch. Stir again for 2 or 3 minutes and season with nutmeg and hot pepper sauce. Place casserole on the table on a hot plate or over an alcohol burner to keep it barely bubbling. Cut bread into bite-size pieces, each with one side of crust. Guests spear pieces of bread on fondue forks and dip them into the cheese. Makes 4 to 6 servings.

QUICHE LORRAINE

France's classic cheese pie, with bacon.

1½ cups grated Swiss
  cheese (6 ounces)
8 slices crisp bacon,
  crumbled
Unbaked 9" pie shell
3 eggs

1 cup heavy cream
½ cup milk
½ teaspoon salt
¼ teaspoon pepper
Dash of cayenne
½ teaspoon dry mustard

Sprinkle cheese and bacon in pie shell. Beat remaining ingredients together and pour into pie shell. Bake in moderate oven (375°F.) 45 minutes, or until firm and browned. Cut in wedges and serve warm. Serves 6.

CHEESE SPINACH PIE

You can cook it in 20 minutes.

Cook and drain 1 box (10 ounces) frozen chopped spinach. Add 1 cup cottage cheese, 2 beaten eggs, 1 teaspoon caraway seed, 1 teaspoon seasoned salt, ¼ teaspoon seasoned pepper and a dash of nutmeg. Put in small shallow casserole or 8" piepan. Sprinkle with 2 tablespoons grated Parmesan cheese and dot with 1 tablespoon butter. Sprinkle with paprika. Bake in moderate oven (350°F.) about 20 minutes. Makes 4 servings.

RICH CHEESE-MACARONI CASSEROLE

8 ounces Swiss cheese,
coarsely shredded
¼ cup grated Romano or
Parmesan cheese
3 tablespoons butter or
margarine
2 tablespoons all-purpose
flour
1 cup milk

1 cup heavy cream, slightly
whipped
½ teaspoon salt
Freshly ground black pepper
to taste
2 cups elbow macaroni,
cooked and drained
Paprika

Put half the Swiss cheese in buttered deep 2-quart casserole and sprinkle with half the Romano cheese. Melt butter in small saucepan, stir in flour and cook over low heat, stirring, 2 minutes. Gradually stir in milk and simmer until smooth and thickened. Fold in whipped cream and add salt and pepper. Pour over macaroni in mixing bowl and toss until well mixed. Pour into cheese-lined casserole. Sprinkle with remaining Swiss and Romano cheeses and, lightly, with paprika. Bake in moderate oven (350°F.) 20 minutes, or until cheese is melted and top is golden brown. Good with fruit salad. Serves 6.

EGGPLANT PARMIGIANA

2 cups olive oil
1 clove garlic, minced
1 large onion, chopped
5 cups canned Italian-style
  tomatoes
½ teaspoon basil
Salt and pepper
1 cup all-purpose flour

2 eggs, beaten
1 cup milk
2 medium eggplants, cut in
  ½″ slices
1 cup grated Parmesan
8 ounces mozzarella cheese,
  diced
¼ cup butter

Heat ¼ cup oil in skillet. Sauté garlic and onion in it until soft. Add next 3 ingredients. Cook, covered, stirring occasionally, 30 minutes. Mix flour, eggs and milk. Dip eggplant slices in mixture; fry in remaining hot oil until just browned. Add more olive oil after each frying. Arrange alternate layers of eggplant, sauce and cheese in casserole, sprinkling each with salt and pepper. Dot with butter; bake in moderate oven (350°F.) 30 minutes. Serves 6 to 8.

GNOCCHI PARMESAN

(Italian Dumplings with Cheese)

½ cup milk
½ cup butter
Salt
1⅓ cups all-purpose flour

5 eggs
Cheese Sauce
Paprika
Grated Parmesan cheese

Heat ½ cup water, the milk and butter to boiling. Add ¼ teaspoon salt and the flour all at once and stir vigorously until mixture leaves the sides of the saucepan and forms a ball. Remove from heat and add eggs, one at a time, beating well after each. Drop a measuring-half-teaspoonful at a time into boiling salted water. When balls come to the surface, remove to a bowl of cold water. Drain well and mix with Cheese Sauce. Put in a shallow baking dish and sprinkle with paprika and ½ cup grated Parmesan cheese. Bake in moderate oven (375°F.) about 30 minutes. Makes 4 servings.

Cheese Sauce Cook 1 small minced onion in 2 tablespoons butter 5 minutes. Blend in 1½ tablespoons flour, ½ teaspoon salt, ¼ teaspoon pepper and a dash of nutmeg. Gradually add 1 cup milk; cook, stirring, until thickened. Remove from heat; stir in ½ cup grated Parmesan cheese.

Gnocchi Mornay Layer drained cooked gnocchi in buttered shallow baking dish with 2 cups Mornay Sauce and ½ cup grated Parmesan or Gruyère cheese. Dot with butter. Bake in hot oven (400°F.) 15 to 20 minutes, or until bubbly-hot and glazed on top.

Mornay Sauce Melt 2 tablespoons butter in saucepan and blend in 3 tablespoons flour. Stir over low heat about 2 minutes, but do not brown. Gradually stir in 2 cups scalded milk. Stir over moderate heat with wooden spoon or wire whisk until mixture comes to full boil. Boil 1 minute, stirring constantly. Season with salt, white pepper or cayenne and a dash of nutmeg. Remove from heat and blend in ⅓ cup grated Swiss or Parmesan cheese, or a mixture of both. Makes 2 cups sauce.

SCALLOPED COTTAGE CHEESE AND ONIONS

A really hearty vegetable dish.

6 medium onions
3 tablespoons butter or margarine
3 tablespoons flour
1 cup milk
1 teaspoon salt

Dash of pepper
¼ teaspoon paprika
1 cup dry cottage cheese
1 green pepper, minced
1 cup soft stale-bread crumbs

Slice onions very thin; cook in boiling water until soft. Melt 2 tablespoons butter and stir in flour. Gradually add milk, stirring until thick. Add next 5 ingredients. Drain onions; arrange in buttered baking dish in alternate layers with cheese mixture and cover with bread crumbs. Dot with remaining butter or margarine. Bake in moderate oven (350°F.) about 20 minutes. Makes 4 servings.

COTTAGE-CHEESE GREEN-NOODLE CASSEROLE

A wonderful accompaniment for cold meats on a buffet table.

¼ pound green noodles
Salt and pepper
1 cup cottage cheese
½ cup dairy sour cream
1 onion, minced
1 small clove garlic, minced

1 teaspoon steak sauce
1 teaspoon seasoned salt
½ cup soft bread crumbs
½ cup shredded Cheddar cheese

Cook noodles in salted boiling water until tender. Drain and mix with next 7 ingredients. Put in shallow 1-quart baking dish. Sprinkle with combined crumbs and cheese. Bake in moderate oven (350°F.) 30 minutes. Makes 4 servings.

MUSHROOM OMELET

½ pound mushrooms, thinly sliced
4 tablespoons butter or margarine

Salt, pepper and paprika
6 eggs

Sauté mushrooms in 2 tablespoons butter 3 to 4 minutes. Add seasonings to taste and keep warm. With fork, lightly beat eggs, ⅓ cup water, ½ teaspoon salt and ⅛ teaspoon pepper. Heat remaining butter in 10″ skillet. Pour in egg mixture; it should set at edges at once. Draw edges toward center with fork so that uncooked portion flows to side and bottom. Tilt skillet to hasten flow of uncooked egg. When egg is set and surface is still moist, increase heat to quickly brown bottom. Remove from heat. Spoon mushrooms evenly in center, and fold sides over filling. Turn out on hot platter and serve at once. Makes 3 to 4 servings.

Corn Omelet Omit mushrooms. Cook 2 tablespoons each green pepper and onion in 3 tablespoons butter 2 or 3 minutes. Add 1 cup cooked whole-kernel corn, ¼ cup heavy cream and salt and pepper to taste; let simmer while preparing omelet. When omelet is done, top with corn mixture. Fold over and put on a hot platter. Sprinkle with ¼ cup grated Cheddar cheese.

Chicken Omelet Omit mushrooms. Heat ¼ cup milk,

¼ teaspoon pepper, 1 can condensed cream of chicken soup, 1 cup diced cooked chicken, 1 teaspoon Worcestershire and ½ cup chopped ripe olives. When omelet is done, cover center with some of the chicken mixture, fold sides over and turn out on hot platter. Top with remaining sauce; sprinkle with parsley.

EGGS BENEDICT

Panfry 8 small thin ham slices until browned and done; keep warm. Split, butter and toast 4 English muffins under broiler. In large skillet, poach 8 eggs in boiling salted water. Top each of 8 muffin halves with a ham slice, then a poached egg. Serve at once with Hollandaise Sauce (page 149) and a garnish of parsley. Makes 4 servings.

SCOTCH EGGS

This savory makes a sumptuous breakfast or brunch, or a lunchbox meal.

4 hard-cooked eggs	Cracker meal
1 egg, beaten	Fat for deep frying
1 pound sausage meat	

Dip eggs in beaten egg. Wrap each in a coat of sausage meat. Dip again in egg. Roll in cracker meal. Fry in hot deep fat (375°F. on a frying thermometer) 5 to 6 minutes. Drain well on paper towels. Makes 4 servings.

HOLLANDAISE SAUCE

In top part of double boiler, beat 3 egg yolks with whisk. Add ¼ teaspoon salt, dash of cayenne and 1 tablespoon lemon juice. Stir in ½ cup melted butter or margarine. Add 3 tablespoons hot water. Put over hot (not boiling) water and cook, stirring, 4 or 5 minutes, or until thickened. Makes about ¾ cup.

FRITTATA ITALIANA
(Italian Omelet)

2 large sweet onions, sliced wafer-thin
4 tablespoons olive oil

Salt and pepper
6 eggs

Sauté onions in half of oil 5 minutes. Season eggs and beat lightly. Stir in onions. Add rest of oil to pan, add eggs and cook over low heat until set. Turn carefully to brown slightly on other side. Makes 4 servings.

HUEVOS RANCHEROS
(Mexican Ranch-style Eggs)

2 tablespoons chopped onion
2 tablespoons olive oil
1 clove garlic, minced
3 chopped canned green chilies
1 teaspoon oregano

1 pound (3 medium) ripe tomatoes, peeled and chopped
1 teaspoon salt
6 eggs
6 crisp-fried tortillas or toast slices

Cook onion in oil until wilted; add other ingredients, except eggs and tortillas, and simmer for 10 minutes. Serve over fried or poached eggs on tortillas. Makes 6 servings.

CHEESE SOUFFLÉ ON BROILED TOMATOES

¼ cup butter or margarine	4 eggs, separated
¼ cup flour	4 large tomatoes, peeled
Salt and pepper	16 rounds buttered toast
1 cup milk	½ pound bacon, cooked
1 cup Cheddar cheese, shredded or in fine pieces	until crisp
	Watercress

Melt butter and blend in flour, 1 teaspoon salt and a dash of pepper. Gradually add milk and cook, stirring, until thickened. Add cheese and stir until melted. Remove from heat, cool slightly, and add well-beaten egg yolks. Cut tomatoes in 4 slices and season with salt and pepper. Broil 1 minute on each side. Transfer tomato slices to toast and arrange in long shallow baking pan. Fold beaten egg whites into cheese sauce and heap each tomato slice with some of the mixture. Bake in hot oven (400°F.) 15 minutes. Garnish with bacon and watercress. Makes 4 servings.

DRIED BEANS, PASTA, RICE

HOW TO BUY DRIED BEANS

Dried beans should be clean, and uniform in size and quality. Since they are usually packaged, a reliable brand will guarantee such beans. Beans come in many sizes and varieties, including limas, black-eye, yellow-eyed, red kidney, pinto, pink, and white beans such as marrow, Great Northern, navy and pea beans.

BEAN STORAGE

After package is opened, beans stored in clean covered container on pantry shelf will keep 1 year. Store cooked beans, covered, in refrigerator 1 to 4 days.

COOKING HINTS

• Fast cooking causes beans to break. Simmering keeps them whole and prevents sticking to bottom of pot.

• A tablespoon of fat added to beans during cooking minimizes foaming.

• Be sure to wait until beans are almost done to add tomatoes, lemon juice, vinegar or wine to beans. The reason: Acid slows down the softening process.

• Cooked beans and bean dishes freeze well.

HOW TO BUY PASTA

The term "pasta" embraces the many kinds of macaroni, spaghetti and noodles that make up the family of flour-paste products. The best quality is made from durum wheat; they don't splinter when broken as do cheaper grades. If noodles contain eggs rather than coloring, it will be so indicated on the label. Always look on the label for pasta products that are enriched with vitamins B_1 and B_2, niacin and iron. Pasta products keep almost indefinitely stored covered on the pantry shelf.

HOW TO BUY RICE

There are a number of different types of rice. Your choice will depend on how you wish to use it. **Regular white milled rice** is washed, cleaned and graded during milling. Use long-grain for salads, stews; short-grain for croquettes, puddings. **Parboiled rice** is preperad by a special process that retains most of the food value, even after milling. **Instant or precooked rice** needs only to steam in boiling water to be ready to serve. **Brown rice** is the whole, unpolished grain of rice with only the inedible hull removed. Its texture is chewy, its flavor nutlike. There are also flavored rices, such as chicken, roast-beef and curry, available in both precooked and cooking styles. Combinations of rice and wild rice (not a cereal), or rice and pasta are also available. Many brands of rice are vitamin-enriched.

RICE STORAGE

Rice, stored covered, keeps almost indefinitely on the pantry shelf. Brown rice is an exception and should be stored, covered, in the refrigerator, as it may become rancid.

BAKED BEANS WITH HAM

1 pound dried beans
1 onion, sliced
2 teaspoons salt
1 smoked ham shank
(3 pounds)
¼ cup catsup

¼ cup light molasses
1 tablespoon vinegar
¼ teaspoon hot pepper
sauce
1 teaspoon dry mustard

Cover washed beans with 6 cups water, bring to boil and boil 2 minutes. Cover and let stand 1 hour; then add onion and salt. Cook until tender. Drain, reserving 1½ cups liquid. Put ham in 3-quart casserole. Put beans around ham and pour liquid mixed with remaining ingredients over top. Cover and bake in slow oven (325° F.) 1½ hours. Remove ham and put beans back in oven. Bake, uncovered, 1 hour. Meanwhile, remove rind from ham and cut meat in bite-size pieces. Add to beans and bake 30 minutes longer. Makes 6 servings.

BLACK BEANS WITH RICE

Cover 1 pound washed dried black beans with 6 cups water, bring to boil and boil 2 minutes. Cover and let stand 1 hour. Cook 1 cup chopped onion, 1 chopped green pepper and 1 minced clove garlic in ½ cup olive oil 5 minutes. Add to beans with 2 bay leaves, 2 teaspoons salt, ¼ teaspoon pepper, 1 smoked-ham bone (optional) and 1 minced slice of bacon. Bring to boil and simmer, covered, 2 hours, adding more water if necessary. Add ¼ cup wine vinegar and serve with hot cooked rice. Garnish with hard-cooked egg and parsley. Makes 6 to 8 servings.

TOMATO-CHEESE SOY BEANS

1 cup dried soy beans
2 cups cooked corn
1 can (19 ounces) tomatoes
1 teaspoon each sugar and seasoned salt
½ teaspoon monosodium glutamate
⅛ teaspoon pepper
1 cup soft bread crumbs
¼ cup melted butter or margarine
½ cup grated Cheddar cheese
Paprika

Cover washed beans with 4 cups water, bring to boil and boil 2 minutes. Cover and let stand 1 hour; then cook until tender. Drain and arrange beans in alternate layers with corn in shallow baking dish. Mix tomatoes, sugar and seasonings; pour over bean mixture. Top with crumbs, drizzle butter over top, and sprinkle with cheese and paprika. Bake, uncovered, in moderate oven (375° F.) about 30 minutes. Makes 6 servings.

CASSOULET

1 pound dried kidney beans
½ pound pork sausage links
1 pound lean lamb, cubed
2 onions, chopped
2 cloves garlic, minced
½ teaspoon dried rosemary
2 teaspoons salt
Dash of pepper
¾ cup red wine

Cover beans with 6 cups water, bring to boil and boil 2 minutes. Let stand 1 hour; then cook, covered, until almost tender. Drain, reserving 1½ cups liquid. Cut sausages in half and fry until browned. Remove sausage. Brown lamb, onion and garlic in fat remaining. Put in 3-quart casserole. Add seasonings and wine. Cover and bake in 350°F. oven 1 hour. Add beans, sausage and bean liquid. Cover and bake 1½ hours. Make 6 servings.

CARUSO SPAGHETTI

2 medium onions, minced
2 tablespoons butter
6 fresh tomatoes, peeled, seeded and chopped
1 cup fat-free beef or veal gravy
¼ cup olive oil
1 can (4 ounces) sliced mushrooms, drained
4 canned artichoke bottoms, diced

1 cup chopped chicken livers
1 teaspoon salt
½ teaspoon pepper
1 teaspoon grated lemon rind
2 tablespoons chopped parsley
12 ounces spaghetti, cooked

Sauté onions in butter until soft and golden. Add tomatoes and gravy; simmer 10 minutes. Heat olive oil and sauté mushrooms, artichoke bottoms and chicken livers about 5 minutes. Add to tomato sauce with next 4 ingredients. Cover and simmer 10 to 15 minutes, stirring frequently. Serve on hot cooked spaghetti. Serves 6.

ITALIAN-SAUSAGE SAUCE

Cut 1 pound sweet or hot Italian sausage in pieces. Cook 10 minutes with ¼ cup water. When sausage begins to brown, add 1 chopped onion and a few sprigs of chopped parsley. Cook until onion is lightly browned. Add ¼ cup water, 1 can (19 ounces) tomatoes, 2 cans (8 ounces) tomato sauce and 1 bay leaf. Simmer, uncovered, 1¼ hours. Season. Serve with grated cheese on 12 ounces spaghetti, cooked. Makes 6 to 8 servings.

LASAGNA

8 ounces lasagna noodles
Salt
1 tablespoon olive oil
1 pound ricotta cheese

8 ounces mozzarella cheese, sliced
Tomato-Meat Sauce
½ cup grated Parmesan cheese

Cook noodles in boiling salted water 25 minutes, or until tender, stirring frequently. Drain and add oil. Arrange in shallow 2½-quart baking dish, making 3 layers each of cooked noodles, ricotta, mozzarella, sauce and grated cheese. Bake in slow oven (325°F.) about 45 minutes. Makes 6 servings.

Tomato-Meat Sauce Brown 1 minced medium onion and 2 minced cloves garlic lightly in ¼ cup olive oil in large skillet. Add 1 pound ground beef and brown lightly. Add 1 can (29 ounces) tomatoes, 1 can (6 ounces) tomato paste, 2 teaspoons salt, ⅛ teaspoon cayenne, 1 teaspoon sugar, pinch of basil, 1 bay leaf and 2 cups water. Simmer, uncovered, about 1½ hours.

TACO CASSEROLE

1 tablespoon bacon fat or
vegetable oil
1 pound ground beef
¾ cup chopped green onion
1 clove garlic, minced
1 can (10½ ounces)
condensed beef consommé
½ cup sauterne
1 can (12 ounces) Mexican-
style corn
1 can (6 ounces) tomato
paste
1 tablespoon chili powder

½ teaspoon ground cumin
4 drops hot pepper sauce
Salt
3 tortillas, each torn in
sixths
¾ cup sharp Cheddar
cheese
1 cup shredded lettuce
1 large avocado, cut in thin
slices
1 medium tomato, cut in
very thin slices

Put bacon fat in skillet, add beef, ½ cup onion and the garlic and sauté breaking up meat with fork, until onions are limp. Add consommé and wine and bring to boil. Simmer 1 minute, then add next 5 ingredients and mix well. Add salt to taste and pour into greased 9" x 9" x 2" baking dish. Poke tortilla pieces into meat mixture and bake, uncovered, in moderate oven (350° F.) about 25 minutes. Remove from oven and sprinkle with cheese. Then top with remaining green onion, the lettuce, avocado and tomato. Serve at once. Makes 4 to 6 servings.

CHINESE FRIED RICE

½ cup diced cooked chicken,
 ham or pork
3 tablespoons butter
1 can (3 ounces) sliced
 mushrooms, drained
1 green onion, chopped

1 pimiento, chopped
1 teaspoon dried green
 pepper
3 tablespoons soy sauce
3 cups cooked rice
1 egg, beaten

Put all ingredients, except last two, in top pan of double boiler over direct heat. When butter is melted, stir in rice lightly with fork. Heat over boiling water. Meanwhile, cook egg in a greased skillet until firm but not browned. Cut in thin strips and put on rice. Makes 4 to 6 servings.

SAUTÉED BROWN RICE AND MUSHROOMS

1 medium onion, minced
¼ green pepper, minced
¼ cup butter or margarine
1 can (3 ounces) mushroom
 stems and pieces, drained

3 cups cooked brown rice
¾ teaspoon salt
½ teaspoon pepper
½ teaspoon chili powder

Sauté onion and green pepper in the butter 5 minutes. Add remaining ingredients and cook until lightly browned, stirring gently. Makes 4 servings.

RISOTTO ALLA MILANESE

¼ cup butter
¼ cup chopped beef marrow
   or 2 tablespoons butter
1 onion, minced
2 cups uncooked rice
½ cup dry white wine

About 5 cups boiling hot
   chicken bouillon
½ teaspoon saffron
⅔ cup grated Parmesan
   cheese
Salt to taste
½ teaspoon white pepper

In heavy saucepan, melt butter and beef marrow. Cook onion until soft but not brown. Add rice and cook 3 or 4 minutes, stirring. (The rice must be transparent, but not brown.) Stir in wine and cook 3 minutes. Add ½ cup boiling bouillon. Cook, stirring, until bouillon is absorbed. Add remaining bouillon ½ cupful at a time, allowing each addition to become absorbed and stirring constantly. It will take 20 to 25 minutes after the first bouillon has been added, depending on the kind of rice used and the degree of doneness desired. Italians eat it *al dente*. After about 15 minutes, steep saffron in a little bouillon and add. When rice is done, stir in cheese, salt and pepper. Serves 4 to 6.

PILAF
(Greek Rice)

1 cup uncooked rice
¼ cup butter

2½ cups chicken stock
1 teaspoon salt

Brown rice in butter. Stir in stock and salt. Cover and simmer gently until stock is absorbed, 15 to 20 minutes. Makes 4 servings.

VEGETABLES

HOW TO BUY FRESH VEGETABLES

When browsing at the fresh-vegetable bins, look for bright color, crisp or firm texture and unwilted unspotted leaves. All fresh vegetables should be young enough to be tender but mature enough to be ripe and full-flavored. They should also be clean, as sand and soil are time-consuming to remove. Usually, vegetables are at their best and cheapest when they are most plentiful. Buy only enough for 1 to 2 days at a time.

VEGETABLE STORAGE

Store potatoes, sweet potatoes, onions and turnips where cool air can circulate around them. Do not clean until ready to use. Generally, sweet potatoes don't keep well, so use promptly. Refrigerate other fresh vegetables at once in plastic bags or vegetable crisper.

VEGETABLE EQUIVALENTS

Corn

16- and 17-ounce cans = about 2 cups kernels
12-ounce can = about 1½ cups
1 box frozen cut = about 1¾ cups kernels
3 medium ears fresh = about 1 cup kernels
6 medium ears fresh = about 1 cup grated or cream-style

Mushrooms

1 pound fresh = 20 to 24 medium mushrooms
1 pound fresh mushrooms, sliced and cooked = 1 can (8 ounces) sliced mushrooms (there will be slightly less in the can)
2 ounces dried mushrooms, soaked in 1½ cups water = 1⅓ cups chopped mushrooms and liquid
1 pound fresh mushrooms = 20 to 24 frozen (do not go by weight)

FRESH-TOMATO TIPS

TO BUY Select firm, plump, smooth tomatoes with good color and without blemishes. If too green, ripen out of the sun in a moderately warm place. Refrigerate just before using. **TO PEEL** Dip tomato in boiling water 1 minute. Cut out stem end and peel with knife. Or hold tomato on fork over heat until skin wrinkles and splits, then peel off skin. *Note* Beefsteak, oxheart, plum and cherry tomatoes need not be peeled.

HOW TO CHOOSE AND STORE FRESH CORN

To choose Look for bright green, snug husks (this denotes freshness) and dark brown silk at the husk end (a sign of well-filled kernels). Milk should flow from kernels when you press them. **To store** Cook fresh corn as soon as possible after buying. Keep in refrigerator until cooking time to preserve tenderness and sweet flavor.

To Freeze Mushrooms

Whole fresh mushrooms frozen by home method tend to water out and be rubbery when cooked. The best way is to cook them first, then freeze. Partially broil large whole mushrooms or sauté button or sliced mushrooms in a little butter or margarine until almost cooked. Cool quickly, then freeze in plastic containers. Cook and label the right amount needed for your recipes.

FAVORITE ITALIAN BROCCOLI

Cook broccoli as usual. Drain; place on serving dish and dress with olive oil, lemon juice and salt and pepper. Good hot or cold. (String beans and cauliflower are also eaten this way. The trick is to dress vegetable while hot so dressing can soak in.)

QUICK SHREDDED BEETS

2 bunches beets
2 tablespoons vinegar
1 teaspoon sugar

2 tablespoons butter or
   margarine
Salt and pepper

Peel beets and shred on coarse grater. Put beets, ¼ cup water, vinegar and sugar in heavy saucepan. Cover and cook 10 minutes, or until beets are tender. Stir twice during cooking. Add butter and season. Makes 4 servings.

BROCCOLI WITH SOUR CREAM

2 pounds fresh broccoli or
   2 boxes frozen broccoli
   spears
Salt
1 cup dairy sour cream

¼ cup mayonnaise
2 tablespoons tomato paste
¼ teaspoon dried basil
2 teaspoons minced drained
   capers

Discard some of the larger leaves and a little of the stalk from fresh broccoli. Put broccoli in saucepan and add 1″ boiling salted water. Cover and cook 10 to 15 minutes. (Cook frozen broccoli as directed on the box.) Drain and cool. Mix ¾ teaspoon salt and remaining ingredients; chill. Serve on broccoli. Makes 4 servings.

SWEET-SOUR RED CABBAGE

1 onion, chopped	3 tablespoons cider vinegar
3 tablespoons butter or margarine	3 tablespoons brown sugar
	1 tablespoon caraway seed
9 cups shredded red cabbage	1¼ teaspoons salt
	¼ teaspoon pepper
1 large tart apple, peeled and diced	⅓ cup seedless raisins

Cook onion in the butter 5 minutes. Add cabbage; cover and cook 5 minutes longer. Add 1 cup water and remaining ingredients, cover and simmer about 10 minutes. Serves 6.

SAUTÉED CORN WITH GREEN ONION

Melt ¼ cup butter or margarine in skillet. Add 4 cups (about 8 ears) cut fresh corn and ½ cup sliced green onions with tops. Cook, covered, over medium heat, shaking skillet occasionally, 5 minutes. Season with salt and pepper. Makes 4 to 6 servings.

RATATOUILLE

This Provençale casserole is as good cold as it is hot.

3 large cloves garlic
1 teaspoon salt
½ to ¾ cup olive oil
2 medium eggplants
1 pound zucchini
8 large tomatoes
3 large green peppers

4 large onions
1 tablespoon salt
Pepper
2 tablespoons minced
   parsley
Oregano or basil

Crush garlic in salt (in a mortar) and put in a Dutch oven or casserole with the olive oil. Peel and dice eggplants, zucchini and tomatoes; dice peppers and chop onions. Put in the casserole in layers, sprinkling the salt, pepper, parsley and oregano between layers. Cook, covered, until vegetables are tender and sauce thick and rich. Correct seasoning if necessary. Makes 12 servings.

BERMUDA CASSEROLE

4 Bermuda onions, cut in
   ¼" slices
6 slices day-old bread
1 cup finely crumbled blue
   cheese
1 cup undiluted evaporated
   milk or light cream

3 eggs, beaten
Salt
Hot pepper sauce
Butter
Paprika

Parboil onion slices in boiling water 10 minutes. Trim crusts from bread and cut bread in small squares. Butter a shallow 1½-quart baking dish. Put onion in dish and cover with bread squares. Sprinkle with the cheese. Mix milk and egg and season with salt and hot pepper sauce. Pour over ingredients in baking dish. Dot with butter and sprinkle lightly with paprika. Bake in moderate oven (375°F.) about 40 minutes. Makes 6 servings.

POTATO-AND-ONION CAKE

4 medium potatoes	Salt and pepper
Butter	Fine dry bread crumbs
3 onions, chopped	

Peel potatoes and slice very thin. Melt butter in heavy skillet. When hot, add alternate layers of potatoes, onions and seasonings. Sprinkle top layer with crumbs. Cook slowly until well-browned on bottom and nearly done. Turn out on flat plate. Add more butter to skillet and slide potato back into pan, brown side up. Cook until browned. Turn out to serve. Makes 4 servings.

HERBED PAN-ROASTED POTATOES

Boil peeled medium potatoes 10 minutes. Drain and arrange around roast of meat about 1 hour before meat is done. Turn occasionally and baste with drippings in pan. When roast is done, remove to hot platter. To brown potatoes more, put under broiler in same pan, turning to brown. Sprinkle with paprika, minced parsley, crumbled thyme or marjoram and arrange around roast.

PANNED MIXED GREENS

Use beet or turnip tops, cabbage, escarole, romaine, chard or spinach.

Cook 2 quarts finely chopped greens quickly in 2 tablespoons bacon fat or margarine in large, heavy saucepan 3 to 5 minutes, stirring constantly. Season to taste. Makes 4 servings.

FRIED TOMATOES, COUNTRY STYLE

6 large beefsteak tomatoes, half-ripe if possible
Salt and pepper
Garlic salt
Fine dry crumbs
2 tablespoons each butter and bacon fat
1 tablespoon flour
½ teaspoon basil
½ teaspoon paprika
1½ cups dairy sour cream
Chopped green onions

Cut tomatoes in ¾" slices. Season with salt, pepper and garlic salt and coat with crumbs. Heat half the butter and fat in large skillet to very hot. Sauté tomatoes quickly on both sides, turning carefully. Remove and reduce heat. Add more fat to pan if needed. Add 1 teaspoon salt and next 3 ingredients, stirring. Add sour cream slowly. Heat over low heat just to thicken. Pour over tomatoes and top with green onion. Makes 6 servings.

SKILLET SQUASH AND ONIONS

2 pounds yellow summer
  squash
3 medium onions, sliced thin

3 tablespoons butter
½ teaspoon salt
¼ teaspoon pepper

Wash squash and dice. Combine all ingredients in skillet. Cover and cook, stirring frequently, 20 to 30 minutes, or until squash and onion are tender. Makes 4 servings.

ZUCCHINI ALLA PARMIGIANA

6 medium zucchini, cut
  lengthwise in ¼" slices
Salt
2 cans (8 ounces each)
  tomato sauce
⅛ teaspoon basil
Pepper

2 eggs, beaten
1 cup seasoned fine dry
  bread crumbs
Vegetable oil
1 cup grated Parmesan
  cheese

Sprinkle zucchini with salt and set aside. Mix tomato sauce, 1 cup water and basil; bring to boil and simmer, uncovered, about 1 hour. Season with salt and pepper. Dip zucchini slices in egg, then in crumbs. Sauté in oil until golden brown on both sides. In greased shallow 1½-quart baking dish, alternate layers of tomato sauce, zucchini and cheese, ending with cheese. Bake in moderate oven (350°F.) about 45 minutes. Serves 6.

SALADS,
SALAD DRESSINGS

SALAD INGREDIENTS

Buy crisp young salad greens. Rinse under running cold water, drain well, wrap in foil or other moisture-proof wrapping and refrigerate. If necessary, dry with a kitchen towel before making salad. If cut fruits that darken are used, moisten them with some of the dressing or a tart juice as soon as cut.

Iceberg and Boston lettuce are the most common types of salad green used. However, a variety of greens is delicious for a green salad. Choose garden lettuce, romaine, bibb lettuce, watercress, escarole, chicory, Chinese cabbage, young dandelion greens, beet greens, spinach or other tender young greens. To vary, add radishes, green onions, chives, tomatoes, fresh herbs, cucumbers, zucchini, celery, red or yellow onion, chard, cauliflower, avocado, carrot, mushrooms or other raw vegetables. Cooked vegetables such as artichoke hearts, peas, string beans, broccoli, tiny Brussels sprouts, beets or asparagus can also be added.

No matter how good the basic ingredients, the salad will be flavorless unless bound together with a well-seasoned dressing. There are also many other ingredients that can be added to salads such as seasoned salt, seasoned pepper, lemon-pepper marinade, dried herbs, garlic and onion salts, celery salt and seed, toasted sesame seed, seasoned croutons and monosodium glutamate.

A salad may be served as an appetizer or first course, as an accompaniment to the main course or as the main course itself, depending on the ingredients. Some fruit salads may also be served as dessert.

CURRIED CHICKEN SALAD

3 cups diced cooked chicken	¾ cup mayonnaise
2 cups finely diced celery	2 to 3 teaspoons curry
⅓ cup slivered almonds,	powder
toasted	1 teaspoon salt
Juice of 1 lemon	⅛ teaspoon pepper
1 tablespoon minced onion	Salad greens

Toss chicken with celery and almonds. Mix remaining ingredients, except greens, and combine with chicken mixture. Chill. Serve on greens. Makes 4 to 6 servings.

CHICKEN BREASTS VÉRONIQUE

4 chicken breasts, boned
before or after cooking
Salt
1 onion, sliced
Dash of hot pepper sauce
1½ cups heavy cream

4 egg yolks
½ cup chopped parsley
2 tablespoons sherry or
Madeira
Watercress
Seedless grapes, halved

Cook chicken breasts in salted water with onion and hot pepper sauce. When tender, remove and cool. Discard skin and cut meat in even pieces. Chill. Place cream and egg yolks in top of a double boiler and stir over hot water until the mixture thickens. Stir in 1 teaspoon salt, the parsley and wine. Spoon the sauce over the chicken and chill. Arrange on serving dish with watercress and garnish with grapes. Good with toasted English muffins, and a peach-melon salad tossed with mustard dressing. Makes 4 servings.

CHICKEN-RICE SALAD

2 cups cooked rice, chilled
2 cups coarsely diced
cooked chicken
1 cup diced celery
2 chopped green onions
1 tablespoon lemon juice

2 tablespoons chopped
green pepper
¾ cup salad dressing or
mayonnaise
Salt and pepper
Salad greens

Mix first 6 ingredients. Add salad dressing and mix lightly. Season to taste. Chill and serve on salad greens. Makes 4 servings.

TARRAGON-VEAL SALAD

Mix 2 cups of diced cooked veal with ¼ cup chopped onion, ¼ cup chopped celery and ½ cup toasted blanched almonds. Blend 1 cup mayonnaise with 1 teaspoon dried tarragon and 1 tablespoon lemon juice. Add enough mayonnaise to veal mixture to bind it. Heap on greens and garnish with remaining mayonnaise, tomatoes, ripe olives and toasted almonds. Serve with herbed French bread. Makes 4 servings.

POTATO-HAM SALAD DELUXE

½ cup dairy sour cream	½ cup diced celery
½ teaspoon salt	2 green onions, thinly sliced
¼ teaspoon seasoned pepper	About 1½ cups diced ham
2 tablespoons each vinegar and milk	½ cup creamed cottage cheese
2 cups diced cooked potato	1 hard-cooked egg, diced
	1 carrot, coarsely shredded

Mix together sour cream, salt, pepper, the vinegar and milk. Combine potato and remaining ingredients, add sour cream mixture and toss lightly. Chill. Makes 4 to 6 servings.

EGG-HAM-MACARONI SALAD

6 eggs, hard-cooked and
diced
1½ cups diced cooked ham
2 cups cooked macaroni,
chilled
½ cup diced celery

1 sour pickle, chopped
¼ cup chopped pimiento-
stuffed olives
Mayonnaise
Salt and pepper
Salad greens

Mix first 6 ingredients. Add mayonnaise to moisten and season to taste. Serve on greens. Makes 4 servings.

SEVICHE

(South American Raw-fish Salad)

1½ pounds lemon sole, cut
in thin strips
1 cup lime juice
½ cup olive oil
¼ cup finely chopped onion
2 tablespoons canned green
chilies, finely chopped
¼ cup finely chopped
parsley

1 clove garlic, finely
chopped
1½ teaspoons salt
1 teaspoon black pepper
Dash of hot pepper sauce
Chopped cilantro (fresh
coriander)

Cover fish strips with the lime juice and refrigerate for 4 hours. Drain. Blend all remaining ingredients, except cilantro, and toss with the fish strips. Chill. Garnish with chopped cilantro. Makes 4 to 6 servings.

Note In South America this dish is often made with tiny scallops or crab meat.

CRAB RAVIGOTE

1 pound lump crab meat
1 teaspoon salt
⅛ teaspoon cayenne
1 teaspoon prepared
  mustard
1 tablespoon olive oil
1 sprig parsley, minced

1 hard-cooked egg,
  chopped
3 tablespoons lemon juice
Ravigote Mayonnaise
Sliced lemon and pimiento
  strips

Gently combine all ingredients, except last 3, and heap in 4 crab shells or ramekins. Chill thoroughly. Just before serving, top with mayonnaise. Garnish with sliced lemon and pimiento strips. Makes 4 servings.

Ravigote Mayonnaise Mix well 1 cup mayonnaise, 1 tablespoon tarragon vinegar, 1 teaspoon finely minced parsley, 1 teaspoon grated onion and a dash of cayenne.

WEST COAST TUNA SALAD

1 large or 2 medium heads
  romaine
2 hard-cooked eggs,
  chopped
3 finely minced green
  onions

1 can (7 ounces) tuna,
  broken up
6 slices crisp, cooked bacon,
  fat reserved
2 tablespoons or more
  wine vinegar
Pepper and salt

Wash romaine, dry and chill; break in pieces into a large bowl. Add next 3 ingredients with bacon, crumbled. Combine vinegar and fresh ground pepper with bacon fat in pan. Heat and pour over salad, mixing gently. Salt if necessary. Makes 6 servings.

COLD SALMON PLATTER

1 can (1 pound) salmon, drained
¾ cup mayonnaise
1 tablespoon lemon juice
1 teaspoon prepared mustard
1 cucumber, peeled
1 large tomato, peeled and cut in wedges
2 hard-cooked eggs, quartered
1 tablespoon chopped fresh dill
Salt and freshly ground pepper
Paprika

Separate salmon in chunks and put in center of platter. Mix next 3 ingredients and spread on salmon. Quarter cucumber, discard seed and cut in thin slices. Arrange with tomato and eggs around salmon. Sprinkle with dill. Season vegetables and eggs lightly with remaining ingredients. Chill. Makes 4 servings.

HOT POTATO SALAD

2 slices bacon
1 onion, chopped
1 tablespoon flour
¼ cup vinegar
½ teaspoon salt
1 teaspoon sugar
⅛ teaspoon pepper
3 tablespoons prepared mustard
5 cups sliced cooked potato
Chopped parsley

Mince bacon and fry until crisp; remove. Cook onion in bacon fat until lightly browned. Blend in flour; add bacon, vinegar, ½ cup water and seasonings; bring to boil. Add potato, mixing lightly; heat. Sprinkle with parsley; serve. Or cool, refrigerate and reheat before serving. Serves 4.

SWEET-SOUR BEAN SALAD

1 cup cooked white kidney beans, drained
1 can (15¼ ounces) red kidney beans, drained
1 can (20 ounces) chickpeas, drained
2 green onions, thinly sliced
½ cup sliced celery
½ green pepper, thinly sliced (or part red pepper or pimiento)
⅓ cup salad oil
½ cup vinegar
3 tablespoons sugar
½ teaspoon salt
⅛ teaspoon pepper
Boston lettuce

Put vegetables in large bowl. Combine remaining ingredients, pour over vegetables and mix gently. Chill several hours or overnight. Serve on Boston lettuce. Makes 6 to 8 servings.

CALIFORNIA CHEF'S SALAD

½ head each lettuce and romaine
½ bunch watercress
1 small bunch chicory
2 tomatoes, peeled, seeded and diced
2 cooked chicken breasts, diced
6 strips crisp bacon, crumbled
1 avocado, diced
3 hard-cooked eggs, diced
2 tablespoons chopped chives
½ cup finely crumbled Roquefort
¾ cup Italian-type dressing

Cut greens in small pieces into large salad bowl. Add remaining ingredients and toss well. Makes 8 servings.

MUSHROOM-RICE SALAD

½ pound mushrooms, sliced
2 cups cooked rice, chilled
1 cup diced tomatoes
½ cup chopped red onion
½ cup chopped green
   pepper
½ cup mayonnaise

1 tablespoon lemon juice
½ teaspoon salt
¼ teaspoon hot pepper
   sauce
Lettuce leaves
Few sprigs of parsley,
   chopped

Combine first 5 ingredients in bowl. Mix mayonnaise with next 3 ingredients and add to bowl. Toss gently. Line salad bowl with lettuce and fill with salad. Sprinkle with parsley. Serve at once or chill 30 minutes. Makes 6 servings.

ITALIAN RAW-MUSHROOM SALAD

½ pound mushrooms
¼ teaspoon each salt and
   pepper

½ teaspoon oregano
3 tablespoons lemon juice
½ cup olive oil

Cut stems ends from mushrooms and reserve for other use. Wipe caps with damp paper towel and slice evenly. Mix remaining ingredients, add mushrooms and toss. Let stand at room temperature about 2 hours. Makes 3 cups.

Note Store any leftovers, covered, in refrigerator.

FRENCH DRESSING

¼ cup each lemon juice and vinegar

1½ cups olive or other salad oil

1 teaspoon seasoned salt

½ teaspoon steak sauce or Worcestershire

¼ teaspoon garlic powder

½ teaspoon sugar

½ teaspoon paprika

Mix all ingredients in 1-quart glass jar, cover tightly and shake until well blended. Refrigerate. Makes 2 cups.

Chiffonade Dressing Mix well ¾ cup French Dressing, 1 tablespoon minced parsley, 2 tablespoons each chopped pimiento and green pepper, 1 teaspoon instant minced onion, 1 finely crumbled hard-cooked egg and 1 tablespoon chopped cooked beet (optional). Makes 1¾ cups.

Herb Dressing To ¾ cup French Dressing, add 2 teaspoons chopped fresh dill, marjoram, rosemary, summer savory or other herbs. Good on greens, seafood or meat.

Vinaigrette Dressing To ¾ cup French Dressing, add 1 chopped hard-cooked egg and 1 teaspoon chopped chives. Good on vegetables or greens.

Deluxe French Dressing To French Dressing recipe, add several split cloves garlic, ⅓ cup chili sauce, 1 tablespoon horseradish and 1 teaspoon paprika.

MAYONNAISE

2 egg yolks or 1 whole egg	2 tablespoons vinegar
1 teaspoon sugar	2 cups olive oil
1 teaspoon dry mustard	2 tablespoons lemon juice
1 teaspoon salt	

Put egg yolks and seasonings in small deep bowl. Beat with rotary beater or electric mixer until blended. Add vinegar very slowly, beating constantly. Add 1 cup oil, 1 tablespoon at a time, beating constantly. Add lemon juice and remaining 1 cup oil, 1 tablespoon at a time. Refrigerate. Makes 2 cups.

Russian Dressing To ½ cup Mayonnaise add ¼ cup chili sauce and 2 tablespoons pickle relish. Good on greens, meat or eggs.

Sharp-Cheddar Dressing Finely shred ½ pound sharp Cheddar cheese; soften at room temperature. Add 1 cup Mayonnaise, 2 tablespoons vinegar, 1 minced clove garlic, ½ teaspoon salt, a dash of cayenne and 2 teaspoons Worcestershire. Beat until blended. Makes about 2 cups. Good on fruit, vegetable, macaroni or potato salad.

Thousand Island Dressing Mix 1 cup Mayonnaise, ½ cup chili sauce, 2 tablespoons minced green pepper, 3 tablespoons chopped stuffed olives, 1 minced pimiento and 1 teaspoon grated onion or 2 teaspoons chopped chives. Makes about 2 cups. Good with seafood, greens, hard-cooked eggs or vegetables.

Green Mayonnaise Mix 2 cups Mayonnaise, ½ cup finely chopped spinach, ¼ cup finely chopped parsley, 2 tablespoons chopped dill or 1 teaspoon dillweed and 2 tablespoons chopped chives.

Roquefort Mayonnaise Beat together to a thick cream 1 cup Mayonnaise, ¾ cup dairy sour cream, ½ pound

Roquefort, crumbled, 1 teaspoon hot pepper sauce and a dash of steak sauce. Makes 2⅔ cups. Good on avocado salad, lettuce wedges or atop baked potatoes.

Spanish Dressing Mix 1 cup Mayonnaise, ¼ cup chopped roasted peanuts, ¼ cup chopped green pepper, ¼ cup chopped ripe olives, 2 tablespoons chopped chives, ½ teaspoon salt and ¼ cup catsup. If too thick, thin with a little white wine. Makes about 1½ cups.

BREADS

HOW TO BUY BREAD

Every family has its own favorite kinds of bread. But whatever the variety, for nutrition's sake, be sure to buy enriched bread, preferably made with milk. Breads made with oatmeal or whole-wheat or rye flour are very nutritious.

BREAD STORAGE

Except in hot humid weather, bread can be kept for a few days in a metal or plastic bread box. Tightly wrapped, bread stored in the refrigerator does not mold quickly but it does lose freshness. Refrigerated bread is satisfactory for toast. All breads freeze well.

TIPS FOR MAKING YEAST BREADS

Yeast Like all plants, the living cells in yeast need water, food, air and heat. They get water and food from other ingredients in any bread recipe; using sifted flour, kneading and beating provide air; the warmth of the water and the temperature of the room provide heat. When yeast becomes active, dough rises.

Kneading Use a board lightly sprinkled with flour. Rub a little flour on your hands. Shape the dough in a round ball and fold it toward you. Using heels of hands, push dough away with rolling motion. Turn one quarter-turn around. Repeat until dough is smooth and elastic.

Rising Doughs need an even temperature of 80°F. to 85°F. for rising. There are several ways to provide a warm place.

1. Set bowl on rack in an unheated oven with large pan of hot water on another rack beneath it.

2. Warm bowl with hot water and dry before greasing it for dough.

3. Fill a large pan two thirds full with hot water, put a wire rack on top and set bowl on it.

4. Set bowl in a deep pan of warm, not hot, water.

5. Put bowl in draft-free place near, not on, range or radiator.

To Speed up Rising Cover bowl with plastic wrap or set whole bowl in a large plastic bag before putting in warm place to rise.

Testing for Double in Bulk Press tips of two fingers lightly and quickly ½″ into dough. If dent remains, dough is double.

Baking When baking bread in glass loaf pans, use an oven temperature 25° less than specified in recipes. This prevents formation of a thick crust (undesirable to some). Baked bread sounds hollow when bottom and sides are tapped with fingers.

Cooling Remove from baking sheet or pans and put on cake racks. Cover with towel for a soft crust; leave uncovered for crisp crust. For extra good flavor, brush hot bread and rolls with soft butter.

Freezing After bread or rolls are thoroughly cooled, wrap in foil, freezer paper, heavy-duty plastic wrap or airtight plastic bags. Press out all air by putting wrap close to bread; seal tightly. Properly frozen bread will retain its freshness for 3 months.

Thawing Thaw in original wrapper and unwrap just before serving.

TIPS FOR COOKING PANCAKES

A dry griddle or cook in fat?

If pancake batter contains enough added fat, it can be cooked on a dry or lightly greased griddle or in a skillet. Where there is little or no added fat (as in bona fide crepes or French pancakes), the batter must be cooked in fat. Do not use too much or pancakes will be greasy. Teflon-coated pans need no greasing.

How to cook pancakes

1. Heat griddle 1 or 2 minutes, or until it is so hot a drop of water will sizzle and bubble away almost immediately.

2. Drop 1 rounded tablespoonful of batter at a time onto griddle, leaving 2″ to 3″ between them to allow for spreading.

3. Turn only once. To check if underside is done, lift edge of cake and see if it is golden brown. Usually, when ready to turn, the top side will be full of bubbles and no longer runny.

4. Do not cook too quickly or outside will burn and inside will be moist. Do not cook too slowly or cakes may become tough.

How to freeze waffles

Cool and wrap each leftover waffle in foil and freeze. Or freeze flat and wrap. To reheat, it is not necessary to thaw. Place each unwrapped section in toaster set at light and toast until section is heated through. These waffle sections become crisp when cool. If you prefer, you can place unwrapped sections side by side on a flat cookie sheet and put under broiler until heated and sufficiently browned. Do not keep over 2 weeks in the freezer.

WHITE BREAD

1 package active dry yeast	2 tablespoons sugar
2 cups milk, scalded	2 teaspoons salt
¼ cup butter or margarine	6 cups all-purpose flour

Sprinkle yeast on ¼ cup warm water. Let stand a few minutes, then stir until dissolved. Pour hot milk over next 3 ingredients. Cool to lukewarm and add yeast and 3 cups flour. Beat well. Add remaining flour and mix well. Turn out on floured pastry cloth or board and knead until smooth and satiny. Put in greased bowl; turn once, cover and let rise until doubled (about 1½ hours). Punch down; let rise ½ hour. Shape in loaves and put in 2 greased 9″ x 5″ x 3″ pans. Let rise until doubled (about 45 minutes). Bake in hot oven (400°F.) about 35 minutes, or until bread is lightly browned on top and done.

Raisin Bread Follow recipe for White Bread but add 1 cup seedless raisins to dough with last addition of flour.

Individual White-bread Loaves Follow recipe for White Bread, but after first rising, cut half of dough in 6 pieces. Shape in small loaves and put in greased 4¾″ x 2⅝″ x 1½″ pans. Let rise until doubled (about 30 minutes). Brush with melted butter and bake in hot oven (425°F.) about 20 minutes. Raise and bake remaining half of dough in greased 9″ x 5″ x 3″ loaf pan.

BATTER ANADAMA BREAD

1 package active dry yeast	2 teaspoons salt
½ cup yellow cornmeal	1 egg
3 tablespoons shortening	2¾ cups sifted all-purpose
¼ cup light molasses	flour

Sprinkle dry yeast into ¼ cup very warm water. Let stand a few minutes; then stir until dissolved. In large bowl of electric mixer stir together ¾ cup boiling water, cornmeal, shortening, molasses and salt. Cool to lukewarm. Add yeast, egg and about half the flour. Blend at low speed, then beat 2 minutes at medium speed. Stir in remaining flour. Spread in greased 9″ x 5″ x 3″ loaf pan. Let rise until batter is 1″ from pan edge. Bake in moderate oven (375°F.) 35 minutes.

Batter Oatmeal Bread Substitute ½ cup rolled oats for the cornmeal.

BUTTERMILK CHEESE BREAD

1 cup buttermilk	½ teaspoon baking soda
⅓ cup butter	1½ cups shredded sharp
¼ cup sugar	Cheddar cheese
2½ teaspoons salt	5 to 5½ cups all-purpose
1 package active dry yeast	flour

Heat buttermilk, butter and 1 cup water until butter melts. Stir in sugar and salt and cool to about 120°F. In large bowl of electric mixer, combine next 3 ingredients with half the flour. Add butter mixture and beat at low speed ½ minute, then beat on medium-high speed 3 minutes. With wooden spoon, stir in more flour to make a soft but firm dough and turn out on floured board. Knead 7 to 10 minutes, or until smooth and elastic. Put in greased bowl and turn greased side up. Cover and let rise in warm place 1 hour, or until doubled. Punch down and shape in 2 loaves. Put in greased 9″ x 5″ x 3″ loaf pans and let rise 30 to 40 minutes, or until doubled. Bake in hot oven (400°F.) 30 to 40 minutes. Turn out on cake racks; cool before cutting.

FRENCH BREAD

1 package active dry yeast	6 cups (about) all-purpose
1 tablespoon shortening	flour
2 teaspoons salt	1 egg white
1 tablespoon sugar	

Sprinkle yeast on ¼ cup warm water. Let stand a few minutes, then stir until dissolved. Pour 1 cup boiling water over shortening, salt and sugar in large mixing bowl. Add ¾ cup cold water and cool to lukewarm. Add yeast and gradually beat in enough flour to form a stiff dough. Turn out on floured pastry cloth or board and knead until smooth and satiny. Put in greased bowl, turn once, cover and let rise until doubled, about 1½ hours. Shape in 2 oblong loaves about 14″ long. Put on greased baking sheets. Let rise about 1 hour, or until doubled. Brush with beaten egg white. With knife, make 3 slashes across top. Bake in hot oven (425°F.) 30 minutes. Reduce heat to 350°F. and bake 20 minutes, or until done.

CINNAMON LOAF

1 package active dry yeast	Butter or margarine
⅔ cup milk, scalded	2 eggs
½ cup sugar	3 cups all-purpose flour
1 teaspoon salt	1½ teaspoons cinnamon

Sprinkle dry yeast into 2 tablespoons very warm water. Let stand a few minutes; then stir until dissolved. Pour hot milk over ¼ cup sugar, the salt and 4 tablespoons butter; cool. Add eggs, yeast and half the flour. Beat with rotary beater or electric beater until smooth. Beat in remaining flour with spoon. Cover and let rise until doubled, about 1 hour. Punch down and knead lightly. Roll out on floured pastry cloth or board to a rectangle 18″ x 9″. Spread with 2 tablespoons butter; sprinkle with ¼ cup sugar mixed with the cinnamon. Roll up tightly from the short end and put in greased 9″ x 5″ x 3″ loaf pan. Brush with 2 tablespoons melted butter and let rise until doubled, about 45 minutes. Bake in moderate oven (350°F.) about 30 minutes.

HONEY-OATMEAL BREAD

(Refrigerator Method)

1½ cups quick-cooking (not instant) rolled oats
⅓ cup honey
¼ cup butter or margarine
1 tablespoon salt
1 cup dairy sour cream

2 packages active dry yeast
2 eggs
4½ to 5 cups all-purpose flour
Honey butter

Combine 1 cup boiling water and first 4 ingredients and stir until butter is melted. Add sour cream and cool to lukewarm. Soften yeast in ½ cup warm water. Add yeast, eggs and 2 cups flour to oat mixture and beat until smooth. Add enough more flour to make a stiff dough. Turn out onto lightly floured board and knead until elastic. Cover dough on board with towel or bowl and let rest 20 minutes. Then divide in 2 equal portions and shape in 2 loaves. Put each in a greased 9″ x 5″ x 3″ loaf pan. Cover pans loosely with plastic wrap and refrigerate 12 to 24 hours. When ready to bake, let stand at room temperature 10 minutes while oven is heating. Bake in moderate oven (375°F.) 50 minutes, or until done. Remove from pans at once and cool on rack. Slice when cold and serve with honey butter (equal parts honey and butter).

LITTLE BRIOCHES

2 packages active dry yeast   2 teaspoons salt
¾ cup milk, scalded   6½ cups sifted all-purpose
1 cup butter or margarine   flour
½ cup sugar   5 eggs

Sprinkle yeast into ¼ cup very warm water. Let stand a few minutes, then stir until dissolved. Pour hot milk over butter, sugar and salt. Cool to lukewarm. Add 2 cups flour and beat well. Add yeast and beat. Cover and let rise until bubbly; stir down. Add 4 eggs and beat well. Add more flour to make a soft dough. Turn out on lightly floured board and knead until smooth and satiny. Put in greased bowl, turn once, cover and let rise 1½ hours, or until doubled. Punch down and divide in 24 pieces. From each piece, make 1 large and 1 small ball. Place large ball in well-greased 2¾" muffin cup. Indent top with thumb; press in small ball. Repeat to fill pans. Let rise 45 minutes, or until doubled. Mix remaining egg and 1 tablespoon water. Brush on rolls. Bake in moderate oven (375°F.) about 15 minutes. Makes 2 dozen.

BOSTON BROWN BREAD

The all-New England favorite.

Cream 2 tablespoons solid vegetable shortening, ¼ cup sugar, 1 egg and ¾ cup molasses; beat. Mix 2¼ cups whole-wheat flour, ¾ cup yellow cornmeal, 1 teaspoon salt and 1½ teaspoons each double-acting baking powder and baking soda; add alternately with 1¾ cups buttermilk to first mixture, beating until smooth. Fold in ⅔ cup seedless raisins. Spoon into 2 well-greased 1-quart molds, filling molds a little more than half full. Cover with greased lids or foil. Set molds on rack in deep kettle and add boiling water to come halfway up sides of molds. Cover and steam about 2½ hours. Makes 2.

SPOON BREAD

This is one of the South's greatest culinary contributions to American cookery. It makes a fine escort for most meats.

1 cup cornmeal	3 eggs, separated
3 cups milk	1 teaspoon double-acting
¾ teaspoon salt	baking powder
¼ cup butter	

Gradually add cornmeal to 2 cups boiling milk in saucepan, stirring with a wire whisk or slotted spoon. Keep stirring until mixture is very thick, switching to a wooden spoon if handy. Reduce heat. Continue cooking until most of liquid has been absorbed. Remove from heat. Add salt, butter and remaining milk beaten with egg yolks. Beat until smooth. Cover and keep at room temperature until ready to bake. Before baking, beat whites until stiff. Fold in baking powder and then fold into the prepared mush. Spoon at once into well-buttered 2-quart baking dish or soufflé dish. Bake in moderate oven (375°F.) 45 to 50 minutes, or until top is golden and mixture no longer shakes in middle when pan is moved. Do not overcook. Serve plain as a starchy vegetable, or top each portion with a teaspoon of tart jelly, such as currant, plum or grape. Makes 8 servings.

Cheesed Spoon Bread Follow above recipe, adding 2 cups shredded sharp Cheddar cheese to the well-blended lukewarm mixture before adding egg whites.

CRANBERRY-NUT BREAD

½ cup butter or margarine
½ cup packed light-brown sugar
¼ cup orange marmalade
¾ cup small-curd creamed cottage cheese (or farmer cheese, mashed)
2 eggs
Grated rind of 1 lemon
Grated rind of 1 orange
¼ cup orange juice
2⅔ cups all-purpose flour

3 teaspoons double-acting baking powder
1 teaspoon baking soda
1 teaspoon salt
¼ teaspoon pumpkin-pie spice
1 cup golden raisins
1 cup cranberries, halved
1 cup coarsely chopped pecans or other nuts
Glaze

Beat first 2 ingredients until fluffy. Add marmalade and next 5 ingredients and mix well. Mix flour and next 4 ingredients and stir into creamed mixture. Fold in fruits and nuts. Spread in well-greased 9″ x 5″ x 3″ loaf pan and bake in slow oven (325°F.) 1 hour and 15 minutes. Brush with Glaze as bread comes from oven. Let stand on cake rack 10 minutes, then remove from pan to rack to cool. Best 1 to 2 days old; can be frozen (omit Glaze; thaw before glazing).

Glaze Mix until smooth 1 cup confectioners' sugar, 1 tablespoon melted butter and about 2 tablespoons orange juice to make a rather thin glaze.

BLUEBERRY MUFFINS

2½ cups all-purpose flour
2½ teaspoons double-acting baking powder
¼ teaspoon salt
Sugar
1 cup buttermilk

2 eggs, beaten
½ cup butter or margarine, melted
1½ cups washed fresh blueberries

Sift first 3 ingredients and ½ cup sugar. Add next 3 ingredients and mix only until dry ingredients are dampened. Fold in berries. Spoon into greased muffin pans; filling two thirds full. Sprinkle with sugar. Bake in hot oven (400°F.) 20 to 25 minutes. Makes 16 to 24 muffins.

TOUCH O' CORN BISCUITS

⅓ cup white or yellow cornmeal
1 cup all-purpose flour
½ teaspoon salt
1 teaspoon sugar
¼ teaspoon baking soda

1 teaspoon double-acting baking powder
⅓ cup solid vegetable shortening
⅓ to ½ cup buttermilk
Butter

Put cornmeal in mixing bowl. Sift remaining dry ingredients over meal. Mix in vegetable shortening with fingers. Add enough buttermilk to make dough suitable for rolling. Make into a ball and roll ⅓" thick on a floured board. Cut with 2" round biscuit cutter. Using a pancake turner, place biscuits on ungreased baking sheet, side by side but not touching. Brush tops with melted butter. Bake in very hot oven (450°F.) 12 to 15 minutes. Serve very hot with butter. Makes about 16.

Note If desired, sprinkle before baking with any seed of your choice, such as poppy, sesame or caraway.

DATE-BRAN BREAD

1 cup all-purpose flour	½ teaspoon baking soda
1 cup whole-wheat flour	½ cup molasses
1½ cups all-bran cereal	1½ cups milk
1 teaspoon salt	1 egg, well beaten
2 teaspoons double-acting baking powder	¼ cup shortening, melted
	1 cup finely cut pitted dates

Mix dry ingredients in bowl. Add remaining ingredients and mix only until dry ingredients are dampened. Pour into greased 9" x 5" x 3" loaf pan and bake in moderate oven (350°F.) about 1 hour. Turn out on rack and cool before cutting.

APPLE-WALNUT GRIDDLE CAKES

2 cups all-purpose flour	2 tablespoons vegetable oil
1 teaspoon baking soda	1½ cups very finely chopped peeled apples
½ teaspoon salt	½ cup chopped walnuts
2 tablespoons sugar	Maple syrup
2 eggs, beaten	
2 cups buttermilk	

Sift dry ingredients. Mix eggs, buttermilk and oil; gradually add to dry ingredients; stir until smooth. Fold in apples and nuts. Bake on hot greased griddle. Serve with syrup. Makes about 20.

CAKES, COOKIES, CONFECTIONS

TIPS FOR MAKING AND BAKING CAKES

Equipment

For easy, accurate measurement, use a set of standard measuring spoons, a nest of measuring cups for dry ingredients and a measuring cup for liquids with a pouring lip and a rim above the 1-cup line. A rubber spatula and a sifter are essential items for preparing batter. Use shiny aluminum or glass baking pans. For layer cakes, use pans about 1½" deep. Waxed paper, plain white or brown paper can be used to line pan bottoms. Cut paper slightly smaller than pan so that it will not touch edge but will completely cover bottom. Greasing the bottom of pan will keep the paper from slipping when batter is poured in.

Procedure

For best results, use only ingredients specified and follow directions exactly. Make all measurements level. Spoon granulated sugar and sifted confectioners' sugar into cup. Level off with flat knife. Do not shake down. Use kind of flour specified. Large eggs were used in making these cakes; substituting eggs of another size is not recommended. You can use either fresh whole milk or evaporated milk diluted with an equal amount of water. Ingredients such as shortening, milk and eggs should be at room temperature (72°F. to 80°F.) It is advisable not to double recipes.

Oven Temperature

Correct oven temperature is of great importance when baking cakes. If your oven has no thermostatic control, try using an oven thermometer and adjusting the heat accordingly. You may want to use a thermometer in any case to check the accuracy of your control. When baking in glass loaf pans, use an oven temperature 25° less than that specified in recipe.

STORING BAKED CAKES

Frosted cakes keep best. It's helpful to store cakes in a cake saver, deep bowl or an airtight container. Cover the cut surface of cake with waxed paper or transparent plastic wrap; hold wrapping in place with toothpicks inserted at an angle into cake. Cakes with perishable fillings or frostings should be stored, covered, in the refrigerator. It is best to freeze cakes unfrosted.

TIPS FOR MAKING AND BAKING COOKIES

Cookie Sheets

You don't have to grease cookie sheets unless the recipe specifies it. Try the new cookie sheets that never need greasing. They come in attractive colors. If you're using aluminum sheets, shiny ones give browner cookies. Choose sheets at least 2″ narrower and shorter than the oven rack so heat can circulate.

Mixing

Measure ingredients accurately. Don't make substitutions such as cocoa for chocolate, or omit ingredients. Don't use self-rising flour. Make cookies of the size specified in the recipe.

When rolling dough, be careful not to work in a lot of flour. For easier rolling, use a pastry cloth or canvas rolling-pin cover. Cut with floured cutter, using a fairly plain one if dough is soft and tender.

Baking

Space cookies to allow for spreading. Because ovens vary, watch cookies closely. Check for doneness just before minimum baking time is up. If some are thinner than others, you may have to remove them and bake the remainder a bit longer.

Cooling

Unless otherwise specified in the recipe, remove baked cookies from the sheet to a cake rack as soon as you take them from the oven. Don't stack them until they have cooled thoroughly.

Storing

Keep cookies in airtight containers. If crisp cookies become limp, heat them a few minutes in the oven to recrisp.

LEMON-ORANGE COCONUT CAKE

1 cup butter
2 cups sugar
3½ cups sifted cake flour
3½ teaspoons double-acting baking powder
¾ teaspoon salt
1 cup milk
2 teaspoons grated lemon rind

1 cup grated fresh coconut or 1 cup canned flaked coconut
6 egg whites
Orange Filling
Lemon-Orange Butter-cream Frosting

Cream butter until soft. Gradually add 1½ cups sugar and beat until light. Add sifted dry ingredients alternately with milk, beating after each addition until smooth. Stir in lemon rind and coconut. Beat egg whites until foamy; gradually add remaining ½ cup sugar and beat until stiff but not dry. Fold into batter. Pour into four 9″ layer cake pans lined on the bottom with waxed paper. Bake in moderate oven (375°F.) 15 to 20 minutes. Cool 5 minutes; then turn out on racks. Peel off paper; cool cakes. Spread filling between layers and frosting on top and sides of cake.

Orange Filling In heavy saucepan, mix ½ cup cake flour, 1 cup sugar and ¼ teaspoon salt. Add ¼ cup water and blend until smooth. Add 1½ cups orange juice, ¼ cup lemon juice, 2 tablespoons grated orange rind and grated rind of 1 lemon. Cook, stirring, until mixture thickens and becomes almost translucent. Beat 4 egg yolks slightly and stir in small amount of hot mixture. Return mixture to saucepan and cook, stirring, a few minutes longer. Cool. Makes filling for four 9″ layers.

MOCHA CAKE

2 squares unsweetened chocolate
1 cup strong coffee
1½ cups packed light-brown sugar
½ cup softened butter or margarine

1 teaspoon vanilla extract
2 eggs
1¾ cups sifted cake flour
1 teaspoon double-acting baking powder
½ teaspoon baking soda
½ teaspoon salt
Caramel Frosting (page 201)

In top of double boiler, cook chocolate and ½ cup coffee until thick, stirring. Add ½ cup sugar and cook 2 or 3 minutes longer, stirring; cool. Cream butter, 1 cup sugar and vanilla. Add eggs, one at a time, beating thoroughly after each addition. Beat in cooled chocolate mixture. Add sifted dry ingredients alternately with ½ cup cold coffee; beat until smooth. Pour into two 9″ layer pans lined on bottom with waxed paper. Bake in moderate oven (350°F.) about 30 minutes. Cool and frost.

CARAMEL FROSTING

In large saucepan mix 2 cups packed light-brown sugar, 1 cup granulated sugar, 2 tablespoons corn syrup, 3 tablespoons butter, a dash of salt, ⅔ cup cream and 1 teaspoon vanilla. Bring to boil, cover and cook 3 minutes. Uncover and cook until a small amount of mixture forms a soft ball when dropped in cold water (236°F. on a candy thermometer). Cool 5 minutes; then beat until thick. If too stiff, add a little hot water. Frosts two 8″ layers.

CHOCOLATE-FUDGE CAKE

Really moist and fudgy.

½ cup butter or margarine, softened
1 cup sugar
1 teaspoon vanilla extract
4 eggs
1 cup minus 1 tablespoon all-purpose flour
1 teaspoon double-acting baking powder
1 can (1 pound) chocolate syrup
1 cup chopped walnuts
Whipped cream, or vanilla or coffee ice cream

Cream butter. Gradually add sugar and vanilla; beat until light. Add eggs one at a time, beating thoroughly after each. Add sifted dry ingredients alternately with syrup, blending well; add nuts. Put in 9″ tube pan lined on the bottom with waxed paper. Bake in moderate oven (350°F.) 35 to 40 minutes. Turn out on rack and peel off paper. Cool and serve with cream.

APRICOT-BRANDY POUND CAKE

1 cup butter or margarine,
   softened
2½ cups sugar
1 teaspoon each vanilla,
   orange and rum extracts
½ teaspoon lemon extract

6 eggs
3 cups all-purpose flour
¼ teaspoon baking soda
½ teaspoon salt
1 cup dairy sour cream
½ cup apricot brandy

Cream butter; gradually add sugar and flavorings and beat until light. Add eggs one at a time, beating thoroughly after each. Add sifted dry ingredients alternately with sour cream and brandy. Blend well. Put in greased 3-quart *bundt* or tube pan and bake in slow oven (325° F.) about 1 hour and 15 minutes. Cool in pan on rack. Store airtight.

MARBLE CHIFFON CAKE

4 squares unsweetened
   chocolate
Sugar
2¼ cups sifted cake flour
2 teaspoons double-acting
   baking powder
1 teaspoon salt

½ cup vegetable oil
7 eggs, separated
1 teaspoon vanilla extract
½ teaspoon cream of tartar
Chocolate Butter-cream
   Frosting (page 203)

Blend 2 squares chocolate, 2 tablespoons sugar and ¼ cup boiling water; set aside. Sift flour, 1½ cups sugar, the baking powder and salt. Make a well in center of dry ingredients; add oil, then egg yolks, ¾ cup cold water and the vanilla. Beat until well blended and smooth. In large bowl, beat egg whites with cream of tartar until very stiff peaks form. Pour egg-yolk mixture in thin stream over entire surface of egg whites, gently folding to blend. Remove one third of batter to separate bowl; gently fold in reserved chocolate mixture. Spoon half of light batter into ungreased 10″ tube pan. Top with half the chocolate batter; repeat. With narrow spatula, swirl gently through batters to form a marbled pattern. Bake in slow oven (325°F.) 55 minutes. Raise temperature to 350°F. and bake 10 minutes, or until done. Invert cake in pan or rack until cold. Remove from pan; spread top and sides with frosting. Melt remaining 2 squares chocolate and cool. Drizzle over top.

CHOCOLATE BUTTER-CREAM FROSTING

Melt 4 squares, unsweetened chocolate in top of double boiler over hot water. Beat 4 egg yolks with ⅔ cup sugar; add ½ cup heavy cream and ⅛ teaspoon salt. Pour slowly over chocolate, stirring constantly. Cook over hot water 5 minutes, or until thickened, stirring. Cream 1¼ cups unsalted butter; add chocolate mixture, 1 tablespoonful at a time, beating until blended. Chill until thick. Frosts 9″ or 10″ tube cake.

COFFEE SPICE CAKE

½ cup butter, softened
1 cup packed light-brown
  sugar
½ teaspoon each vanilla
  and lemon extracts
2 eggs
1⅓ cups all-purpose flour
1½ teaspoons double-acting
  baking powder
½ teaspoon salt
1 teaspoon cinnamon
¼ teaspoon each ginger,
  cloves and nutmeg
⅓ cup undiluted evaporated
  milk
¼ cup strong coffee
Coffee Frosting (below)

Cream butter, sugar and flavorings until light. Add eggs, one at a time, beating well after each addition. Add sifted dry ingredients alternately with milk and coffee, beating until smooth. Pour into 9" x 9" x 2" pan lined on the bottom with waxed paper. Bake in moderate oven (350°F.) 25 to 35 minutes. Cool and frost.

COFFEE FROSTING

Cream ⅓ cup butter. Add a dash of salt and ½ teaspoon vanilla. Gradually beat in 2½ cups sifted confectioners' sugar and enough strong coffee (about 2 tablespoons) for spreading consistency. Frosts two 8" layers.

MELT-IN-THE-MOUTH COOKIES

½ cup butter
1 cup packed light-brown
sugar
1 teaspoon vanilla extract
1 egg

¾ cup all-purpose flour
1 teaspoon double-acting
baking powder
½ teaspoon salt
½ cup finely chopped nuts

Cream butter and add next 3 ingredients; beat until light. Add sifted dry ingredients and nuts. Drop by scant measuring-teaspoonfuls onto cookie sheets. Bake in hot oven (400°F.) about 5 minutes. Cool ½ minute. Remove to racks. Store airtight. Makes about 8 dozen.

BUTTERSCOTCH CRISPS

1 package (6 ounces)
butterscotch pieces
⅓ cup butter
¼ cup sugar
¼ cup corn syrup
1 egg

1 teaspoon vanilla extract
2 cups sifted all-purpose
flour
1 teaspoon baking soda
¼ teaspoon salt
Nut halves

Combine butterscotch pieces, the butter, sugar and corn syrup in saucepan. Put over medium heat, stirring until pieces melt. Cool 5 minutes. Beat in egg and vanilla. Add sifted dry ingredients and mix well. Drop by measuring-teaspoonfuls on cookie sheet. Put piece of walnut in center of each. Bake in moderate oven (350° F.) 8 minutes. Makes 6 dozen.

SAND TARTS

1 cup softened butter or
   margarine
1 cup sugar
2 tablespoons brandy
1 egg

1 package (6 ounces)
   semisweet chocolate
   pieces, ground
1⅞ cups all-purpose flour
⅛ teaspoon salt

Cream butter and sugar with brandy until light; beat in egg. Add remaining ingredients and mix well. Drop by teaspoonfuls on ungreased cookie sheets and bake in moderate oven (350°F.) about 15 minutes. Makes about 7 dozen.

ROLLED BRANDY WAFERS

½ cup molasses
½ cup butter
1½ cups sifted cake flour
¼ teaspoon salt

⅔ cup sugar
1 tablespoon ginger
3 tablespoons brandy

Heat molasses to boiling; add butter. Add sifted dry ingredients gradually, stirring constantly. Stir in brandy. Drop by half-teaspoonfuls 3″ apart onto greased cookie sheets. Bake, 6 cookies at a time, in slow oven (300°F.) 8 to 10 minutes. Cool 1 minute. Remove with spatula; roll at once around handle of wooden spoon. Store airtight. Makes about 5 dozen.

OATMEAL LACE COOKIES

1 cup softened butter
⅔ cup sugar
1 teaspoon grated orange
  rind
½ teaspoon vanilla extract
2 eggs

½ cup sifted all-purpose
  flour
½ teaspoon salt
1 cup rolled oats
½ cup flaked coconut

Cream butter; gradually beat in next 3 ingredients. Add eggs, one at a time, beating well after each addition. Add remaining ingredients. Drop by half-teaspoonfuls onto buttered cookie sheets; flatten with knife dipped in cold water. Bake in moderate oven (350°F.) 10 to 12 minutes, or until edges are lightly browned. Do not overbake. Store airtight. Makes 96.

CHRISTMAS FUDGE

⅔ cup (1 small can)
  undiluted evaporated milk
2 tablespoons butter or
  margarine
1⅔ cups sugar
½ teaspoon salt
2 cups (4 ounces) miniature
  marshmallows

1½ cups (9 ounces) semi-
  sweet chocolate pieces
½ cup chopped pistachio
  nuts
¼ cup crushed peppermint
  sticks

Mix first 4 ingredients in saucepan. Bring to boil and cook 4 to 5 minutes, stirring constantly. (Begin timing when mixture bubbles.) Remove from heat and add next 3 ingredients. Stir briskly until marshmallows are melted. Pour into buttered 8″ square pan and sprinkle with candy. Cool thoroughly until firm and cut in squares. Makes about 2 pounds.

SPICED MIXED NUTS

1½ cups unsalted mixed nuts
¼ cup vegetable oil
2 cups sifted confectioners' sugar
1½ tablespoons egg white, slightly beaten
½ teaspoon each ginger and nutmeg
½ teaspoon cinnamon
1½ teaspoons brandy flavoring

Put nuts on cookie sheet and heat in moderate oven (350°F.) about 15 minutes. Meanwhile, blend remaining ingredients. Stir in nuts, coating nuts thoroughly. Spread out on cool cookie sheet to dry. Separate nuts. Makes about 2½ cups.

NUT BRITTLE SQUARES

Butter the outside bottom of an 8″ square pan and sprinkle evenly with 1 cup rather finely chopped Brazil nuts, filberts, California walnuts, pecans, peanuts or other nuts. Set pan, nut side up, on a tray. Put 1 cup sugar in heavy skillet and heat, stirring, until golden brown and syrupy. At once pour evenly over nuts. When slightly cooled, remove in one piece and cut in 2″ squares. Makes ½ pound.

DESSERTS, SAUCES

THE APPROPRIATE DESSERT

A good dessert can be the happy climax to a meal and can also help to round it out nutritionally. If the day's menus have been short on milk, eggs or fruits, the omission can be rectified by dessert at dinner. The dessert should be geared to the rest of the meal and can supplement a light meal or add a delicate finish to a heavier one. The high point of a light meal might be a gorgeous cheesecake. Fruit is often the best choice, and a basket or bowl of fresh fruit can be used as a centerpiece as well. Cheese and crackers go well with a ripe pear or apple. Ice cream is convenient, wholesome and universally popular.

CRANBERRY-APPLE CRISP

Serve warm with cream or vanilla ice cream.

2 cups fresh cranberries
3 cups coarsely chopped
   peeled apples
1 cup granulated sugar

1½ cups rolled oats
1 cup packed brown sugar
½ cup butter or margarine
½ teaspoon salt

Combine first 3 ingredients. Turn into buttered 9"
piepan or 8" square baking dish. With pastry blender or
fingertips, work together remaining ingredients to make
a crumbly mixture. Sprinkle on fruit. Bake in moderate
oven (350°F.) 1 hour. Makes 6 to 8 servings.

CHOCOLATE SOUFFLÉ

2 squares unsweetened
   chocolate
2 cups milk
½ cup sugar
⅓ cup flour
½ teaspoon salt

2 tablespoons butter or
   margarine
1 teaspoon vanilla extract
4 eggs, separated
Sweetened whipped cream

Melt chocolate in milk in top part of double boiler
over boiling water. Beat until blended. Mix sugar, flour
and salt; stir in small amount of chocolate mixture. Return to double boiler and cook, stirring, until thickened;
cook 5 minutes longer. Remove from heat and stir in
butter and vanilla; cool slightly. Beat egg whites until
stiff. Beat egg yolks until thick and lemon-colored. Stir
yolks into chocolate mixture; fold in whites. Pour into

buttered 1½-quart soufflé dish or casserole. Put in pan of hot water and bake in moderate oven (350°F.) 1 hour and 15 minutes, or until firm. Serve at once with whipped cream. Serves 6 to 8.

SWEDISH PANCAKES WITH LINGONBERRY CREAM

(Plattar med lingongradde)

A Swedish pancake pan is cast-iron with seven ¼"-deep depressions 3" in diameter. It is necessary, since batter is runny and must be held in molds.

1 cup all-purpose flour	¼ cup butter or margarine,
2 tablespoons sugar	melted
¼ teaspoon salt	½ cup heavy cream,
3 eggs, beaten	whipped
3 cups milk	½ cup lingonberry preserves

Mix flour, sugar and salt. Mix eggs and milk and add to dry ingredients. Heat Swedish pancake pan slowly. Brush individual sections of hot pan with melted butter. Stir batter, then put about 1 measuring-tablespoonful into each section. Brown on both sides. Pile pancakes on top of each other and transfer to hot serving platter. Keep platter warm over pan of boiling water. Mix whipped cream and preserves and serve with pancakes. Makes 8 servings.

Note Pancakes can be served with sugar and other preserves instead of whipped cream and lingonberry preserves.

BLUEBERRY BUCKLE

¼ cup butter
¾ cup sugar
1 egg
2 cups all-purpose flour
2 teaspoons baking powder

½ teaspoon salt
½ cup milk
2 cups washed fresh
  blueberries
Crumb Topping

Cream butter, add sugar and beat until light. Add egg and beat well. Add sifted dry ingredients alternately with milk, beating until smooth. Fold in berries. Sprinkle with Crumb Topping. Bake in greased 9" x 9" x 2" pan in moderate oven (375°F.) about 35 minutes. Makes 6 to 8 servings.

Crumb Topping Blend ¼ cup soft butter, ½ cup sugar, ⅓ cup all-purpose flour and ½ teaspoon cinnamon.

CUSTARD RICE PUDDING

½ cup cooked rice
3 eggs, beaten
½ cup sugar
¼ teaspoon salt
1 teaspoon vanilla

1½ teaspoons grated lemon
  rind
½ cup raisins
3½ cups milk
Nutmeg

Mix all ingredients, except nutmeg. Pour into shallow baking dish and sprinkle with nutmeg. Set in pan of hot water and bake in slow oven (300°F.) about 1½ hours. Serve warm or cool, plain or with a sauce. Makes 6 servings.

APPLE PANDOWDY

3 cups sliced apples
⅓ cup packed brown sugar
¼ teaspoon each cinnamon
   and nutmeg
¼ cup butter or margarine
⅓ cup granulated sugar

1 egg
¾ cup all-purpose flour
¾ teaspoon baking powder
¼ teaspoon salt
⅓ cup milk
Cream

Put apples in 1-quart baking dish. Sprinkle with brown sugar and spices. Bake in moderate oven (375° F.) 30 minutes, or until apples are soft. Cream butter; gradually add granulated sugar and beat until fluffy. Add egg and beat well. Add sifted dry ingredients alternately with milk, beating until smooth. Spread on cooked apples. Bake 30 minutes. Serve warm with cream. Makes 4 servings.

BAKED INDIAN PUDDING

A traditional, long-baking New England pudding.

4 cups milk
5 tablespoons yellow
   cornmeal
2 tablespoons butter
½ cup packed brown sugar
½ cup molasses
1 teaspoon salt

½ teaspoon each ginger,
   cinnamon, nutmeg and
   mace
2 eggs, beaten
1 cup light cream
Vanilla ice cream

In top part of double boiler over direct heat, bring to boil 3 cups milk. Mix 1 cup cold milk with cornmeal and stir slowly into hot milk. Put over boiling water and cook 20 minutes, stirring occasionally. Add butter, sugar and molasses. Remove from heat and add salt and spices. Stir in eggs and pour into 1½-quart baking dish. Bake in slow oven (300°F.) 2 to 2½ hours, stirring occasionally the first hour. Then pour light cream over top and finish baking without stirring. Serve warm with ice cream. Makes 6 to 8 servings.

ZABAGLIONE

5 egg yolks
¾ cup sugar
⅛ teaspoon salt

½ cup Marsala, port or
sherry wine

In top of a double boiler, beat egg yolks with 1 tablespoon water until they are foamy and light. Whisk in sugar, salt and wine. Beat a few minutes over hot, not boiling, water until thickened and fluffy. Pile into sherbet glasses; serve hot. Makes 6 servings.

Zabaglione with Fresh Strawberries or Peaches Prepare Zabaglione. Cool and fold in 5 stiffly beaten egg whites. Pile in a pretty serving bowl and garnish with sliced and sweetened fresh fruit.

Chocolate Sabayon Prepare Zabaglione. Stir 2 ounces grated sweet chocolate into hot dessert just before serving.

Frozen Sabayon Prepare Zabaglione. Cool and add 1 pint heavy cream, whipped, ¼ cup diced candied cherries, ½ cup diced candied pineapple and ½ cup chopped pecans. Freeze in parfait glasses and garnish with candied cherries and bits of angelica. Or pour into trays or mold and freeze. Makes 10 to 12 servings.

FRESH FRUIT COMPOTE

1 cup sugar
1 lemon, sliced
4 firm peaches, peeled and
   halved

4 pears, peeled, cored and
   halved
4 plums (see Note)
8 apricots

Put the sugar, lemon and 2 cups water in saucepan, bring to boil and simmer 5 minutes. Add peaches and pears, cover and simmer 5 minutes. Prick skins of plums and add with apricots to mixture. Cover and simmer 5 minutes, or until all fruit is tender. Cool, then chill. Makes 8 servings.

Note If purple plums are used, cook separately in a little syrup and add just before serving.

SCOTCH TRIFLE

1 sponge layer
1 cup strawberry, raspberry
   or other jam
6 macaroons
⅓ cup cream sherry or
   Marsala
⅓ cup orange juice or fruit
   syrup

Soft Custard
1 cup heavy cream, whipped
¼ cup sugar
1 teaspoon vanilla extract
¼ teaspoon almond extract
2 tablespoons chopped
   toasted almonds
Fresh strawberries (optional)

Split the sponge layer in half horizontally and spread thickly with jam. Cut in small fingers. Crumble the macaroons. Arrange alternate layers of sponge fingers and crumbled macaroons in a glass serving dish. Sprinkle each layer with sherry and fruit juice. Pour the cooled custard over the trifle. Cover and chill. At serving time whip cream and add sugar and extracts; spread over the chilled trifle. Sprinkle with chopped nuts and decorate with fresh strawberries, if desired. Makes 6 to 8 servings.

Soft Custard In top part of small double boiler, beat together with rotary beater 2 eggs, dash of salt, 3 tablespoons sugar and 1½ cups milk. Cook over simmering water, stirring, until slightly thickened. Cool.

PEARS MOCHA

1 can (29 ounces) pear halves	semisweet chocolate pieces, melted
1½ teaspoons instant-coffee powder	½ teaspoon vanilla extract
1 package (6 ounces)	½ cup heavy cream, whipped
	¼ cup chopped walnuts

Drain pears, reserving syrup, and chill. Dissolve coffee powder in ¼ cup hot pear syrup and add to chocolate. Beat until cool and smooth but not firm. Fold with vanilla into whipped cream. Arrange pear halves in 4 to 6 dessert dishes, top with chocolate mixture and sprinkle with nuts. Serve at once. If desserts must stand, chill pears and sauce separately. If sauce becomes too thick, thin with a little pear syrup. Makes 4 to 6 servings.

STRAWBERRY CHANTILLY

1 quart strawberries
2 cups heavy cream
½ cup grated sweet cooking chocolate

2 tablespoons sifted confectioners' sugar
2 tablespoons light rum

Hull berries and arrange in bowl. Whip cream until foamy and barely thickened. Fold in chocolate, confectioners' sugar and rum; chill. Serve as sauce for strawberries. Makes 6 servings.

LEMON MOUSSE IN ORANGE SHELLS

6 oranges
4 eggs, separated
½ cup sugar
Grated rind of 1 lemon

3 tablespoons lemon juice
1 cup heavy cream, whipped
Minted Leaves and Stems, (page 218)

Slice off tops of oranges about 1" down from stem end and reserve. Using a small sharp knife, remove pulp from oranges and cut in small pieces, discarding white membrane. (Drain off juice and reserve for other use.) Beat egg yolks until thick; beat in next 3 ingredients. Put in top part of double boiler over simmering water and cook, stirring, 5 minutes, or until very thick. Put in large bowl to cool. Fold in stiffly beaten egg whites, cream and orange pieces. Spoon about ½ cup mixture into each orange cup. Chill several hours. Arrange 2 minted leaves and a stem on each orange top and place on oranges. Makes 6 servings.

MINTED LEAVES AND STEMS

In mixing bowl, beat ¼ cup small-curd creamed cottage cheese and 3 cups sifted confectioners' sugar. Add more sugar if needed to make a stiff workable mixture. Tint a delicate shade of green. Flavor with ¼ teaspoon peppermint or wintergreen extract. Knead stiff mixture several turns. Sprinkle board generously with granulated sugar. Cover mixture with a piece of waxed paper and roll to about ½" thickness. Remove paper, turn mixture over and roll to ¼" thickness. With small knife, cut leaves and make indentations to resemble veins. Roll small balls to make stems.

SNOW PUDDING WITH STRAWBERRY SAUCE

1 envelope unflavored
  gelatin
¾ cup sugar
⅛ teaspoon salt
Grated rind of 1 lemon

¼ cup lemon juice
3 egg whites
Strawberry Sauce
Toasted sliced almonds

Soften gelatin in ¼ cup cold water. Add ½ cup sugar, the salt and 1 cup boiling water; stir to dissolve gelatin and sugar. Add rind and juice and chill until partially set. Beat egg whites until almost stiff; gradually add remaining ¼ cup sugar, beating until stiff. Add gelatin mixture and beat until well blended. Chill until firm. Using large serving spoon, mound in glass serving bowl, drizzle sauce on top and sprinkle with nuts. Makes 6 to 8 servings.

Strawberry Sauce Wash, hull and slice 1 pint strawberries and purée in blender or by hand. In top part of double boiler, mix 3 egg yolks, 3 tablespoons sugar, ¼ cup water and strawberry purée. Cook, stirring, over hot water until thickened and foamy. Flavor with ½ teaspoon strawberry extract; chill. If too pale, tint with a few drops red food coloring, if desired.

SANDWICHES

BREAD FOR SANDWICHES

Hot or cold, at home, school or office, sandwiches are a national lunchtime favorite. Choose the bread carefully. Packaged sliced bread is fine for picnic or lunchbox sandwiches, but for tea or cocktail sandwiches, unsliced bread is best. It should be at least 24 hours old to slice easily. Ready-cut slices can be sliced again with a thin sharp knife. Varying the kind of bread avoids monotony for those who eat sandwiches frequently. Choose whole-wheat, raisin, oatmeal, rye, Boston brown bread, cracked-wheat, pumpernickel, nut bread, orange bread, hero loaves, seeded and sandwich rolls.

SANDWICH STORAGE

Keep prepared sandwiches well covered and refrigerated until time to serve them. Plates of sandwiches can be covered with waxed paper, foil or plastic, wrapped in a damp cloth and refrigerated. Waxed-paper or plastic envelopes are convenient for enclosing individual sandwiches.

SANDWICH FILLINGS

Many prepared fillings are available: deviled ham; luncheon-meat spread; corned-beef spread; liver pâté; cream cheese with pimientos, with olives and pimientos, with pineapple, with chives and with Roquefort; chicken spread; chipped-olive spread; blue-cheese spread; bacon-cheese spread; smoke-flavored cheese spread and many others. Hot meat and poultry sandwiches can be varied by serving them open-faced with sauce or gravy such as cheese sauce, meat-loaf sauce, tomato sauce, sour-cream sauce, spaghetti sauce, curry sauce, brown or mushroom gravy or à la king sauce. Many sauces and gravies are available in cans or packages.

FOR A CROWD

1 medium head of lettuce averages 16 leaves. 1 pint of mayonnaise spreads about 50 average slices of bread if you use 1½ teaspoons (½ tablespoon) per slice. 1 pound of softened butter or margarine spreads

about 96 slices if you use 1 teaspoonful per slice. 1 pound of cheese averages 16 slices.

LIVER-AND-BACON SANDWICHES

Cook 8 slices bacon until crisp. Remove bacon and pour off some of the fat. With fork, prick 1 pound chicken livers. Cook in fat until browned on both sides. Force through food chopper, using medium blade; put bacon and 1 peeled small onion through food chopper. Add 2 tablespoons prepared mustard and enough mayonnaise or salad dressing to moisten. Season to taste with salt and pepper. Spread between 8 slices bread. Serve with tomato wedges. Makes 4 servings.

TENNESSEE SLOPPY JOES

1 pound ground beef
1 medium onion, chopped
½ cup diced celery
¼ cup chopped green pepper
3 tablespoons catsup

2 tablespoons Worcestershire
Dash of hot pepper sauce
Salt and pepper to taste
Toasted sandwich rolls

Brown meat lightly in skillet, breaking up with fork. Pour off excess fat. Add 1 cup water and remaining ingredients, except rolls. Bring to boil, cover and simmer 20 minutes, adding more water if necessary. Serve on rolls. Makes 4 servings.

FRANKFURTERS IN BISCUITS

1½ cups all-purpose
   buttermilk biscuit mix
Prepared mustard

8 frankfurters (about
   1 pound)
Pickles (optional)

With fork, stir biscuit mix and ⅓ cup water to form soft dough. Gently smooth in a ball on floured board and knead 5 turns. Roll in 12″ circle and cut in 8 wedges. Spread each with mustard. Make a slit in each frankfurter and insert a thin strip of pickle, if desired. Put a frankfurter on each wedge and roll up, beginning at wide end. Put on ungreased baking sheet and bake in very hot oven (450°F.) about 15 minutes. Delicious hot or cold. Makes 8.

CORNED-BEEF SANDWICHES
WITH MUSTARD DRESSING

Spread 8 large slices rye bread with prepared mustard, then cover with thinly sliced corned beef and overlapping thin Cheddar-cheese slices. Spread with Mustard Dressing to within ½″ of edges. Put under boiler until dressing is bubbly and cheese is melted. Garnish with pimiento strips, if desired. Makes 8 sandwiches.

Mustard Dressing Mix thoroughly 1 cup mayonnaise, 3 tablespoons prepared mustard, 1 tablespoon prepared horseradish, 1 teaspoon Worcestershire, ½ cup well-drained pickle relish and a dash of hot pepper sauce.

HE-MAN LONGBOY

A meal in itself with meat, vegetables and cheese.

1 long thick loaf French or Italian bread	½ pound thinly sliced cooked ham
1 clove garlic, cut	Chicory
Softened butter or margarine	2 large firm ripe tomatoes, cut in thick slices
½ pound sliced bologna	1 large Spanish onion, thinly sliced
½ pound sliced Italian salami	12 slices Muenster cheese
½ pound sliced cooked smoked tongue	6 strips crisp bacon
	Green olives

Slice off top third of loaf horizontally. Rub cut sides of both pieces with garlic and spread with softened butter. On bottom piece, arrange layers of meat, vegetables and cheese. Garnish with bacon and olives. Cut in serving pieces; cut top piece to match and arrange on longboy. Good served with pickle relish, mustard, dill pickles, pickled red peppers, French dressing and potato sticks. Makes 6 to 8 servings.

BAKED TUNA-CHEESE LOAF

1 can (7 ounces) tuna,
drained
1 teaspoon instant minced
onion
2 tablespoons chopped
sweet pickle
1 cup grated sharp Cheddar
cheese

1 loaf French or Italian
bread (about 12″ long)
¼ cup butter or margarine
1 teaspoon prepared
mustard or ¼ teaspoon
dry mustard

Mix first 4 ingredients. Cut bread in half lengthwise. Remove a small amount of the crumbs. Spread inside with butter, mustard and tuna filling. Put loaf together, wrap in foil and bake in moderate oven (350°F.) about 20 minutes. Cut in 4 crosswise pieces.

INDIVIDUAL TUNA PIZZAS

⅓ cup mayonnaise
½ teaspoon salt
¼ teaspoon each dried
oregano and basil
1 teaspoon instant minced
onion
½ cup finely diced celery

2 cans (7 ounces each) tuna,
drained
8 English-muffin halves or
6 slices toast
½ can (8-ounce size) tomato
sauce
Grated Parmesan cheese

Mix all ingredients, except muffins, sauce and cheese. Pile on muffins. Spoon tomato sauce on top and sprinkle with cheese. Put under broiler until heated and lightly browned. Makes 4 servings.

SMOKED-SALMON ROLLS

Slice white bread thin and remove crusts. Cover with sliced smoked salmon and sprinkle with freshly ground black pepper. Roll up, fasten with picks at each end and grill until bread is lightly browned.

TRIPLE-DECKER EGG-SALAD SANDWICHES

5 hard-cooked eggs
3 tablespoons mayonnaise
2 tablespoons minced sweet
  pickle
½ teaspoon pepper
12 slices white bread
6 slices tomato

6 slices whole-wheat bread,
  buttered
2 cans (4½ ounces each)
  sardines in oil, drained
Lemon juice
Butter

Chop 4 eggs. Cut remaining egg in 6 slices. Mix chopped egg with mayonnaise, pickle and pepper. Spread on 6 slices white bread. Top with tomato slices. Cover with wholewheat bread, then egg slices and sardines. Sprinkle with lemon juice and top each sandwich with white bread, spread with butter. Makes 6 large sandwiches.

SWISS-CHEESE, EGG AND
ANCHOVY SANDWICHES

¼ cup soft butter or margarine
3 tablespoons very finely chopped watercress
1 teaspoon lime juice
Dash of hot pepper sauce
8 large slices rye or whole-wheat bread
4 hard-cooked eggs, chopped

1 can (2 ounces) flat anchovies, drained and mashed
1 teaspoon instant minced onion
¼ teaspoon dry mustard
¼ cup mayonnaise or salad dressing
4 slices Swiss cheese

Blend first 4 ingredients. Spread on 4 slices bread. Mix next 5 ingredients and spread on remaining bread. Top with cheese and cover with watercress-buttered bread. Makes 4.

HOT CHEESE-CHICKEN SANDWICH, LA SALLE

6 slices white bread
6 tablespoons butter
Thin slices of cooked chicken
½ cup blue or Roquefort cheese crumbled
3 tablespoons flour
¾ teaspoon salt
¼ teaspoon pepper

¼ cup heavy cream
1¾ cups milk
1 teaspoon instant minced onion
2 egg yolks, beaten
¼ cup grated Parmesan or Romano cheese

Cut crusts from bread and spread slices with 2 tablespoons butter. Arrange flat in shallow baking dish. Top with chicken and sprinkle with crumbled cheese. Melt remaining butter and blend in flour and seasonings. Add liquids and onion and cook, stirring, until thickened. Stir small amount into egg yolks. Return mixture to saucepan and cook 2 to 3 minutes, stirring. Pour over ingredients in baking dish. Sprinkle with grated cheese. Bake in hot oven (425°F.) 15 minutes, or until golden brown. Serves 6.

CHICKEN CLUB SANDWICHES

18 slices white bread, trimmed
Softened butter or margarine
Lettuce
24 tips chilled cooked asparagus
6 large slices chilled cooked chicken breast
Salt and pepper
Mayonnaise
24 slices crisp bacon
6 chilled hard-cooked eggs, sliced

Spread bread with butter. Cover 6 slices of bread with lettuce, asparagus and chicken. Season. Cover each with bread slice, buttered side down. Spread top side with mayonnaise. Cover with bacon and egg slices. Top with remaining bread, buttered side down. Cut sandwiches in quarters. Makes 6 sandwiches.

PIES, PASTRIES

FOR PERFECT PIE CRUST

Some people say a pie is only as good as its crust.
The pastry should be tender, golden brown and taste
of good fat. If you are an amateur at pie-making, make
a good but simple filling and concentrate on the pastry.
This chapter offers a number of recipes for pie crust;
choose the one that is most convenient for you (or use
one of the many good pie-crust mixes on the market).
Before starting to make pastry, be sure that you have
the right equipment—a board, rolling pin, wire pastry
blender, mixing bowl, measuring cups and spoons, canvas cover for the board and stockinet cover for the
rolling pin. Select a regulation piepan with a slanting
rim. A pan measuring 8″ across the top will hold
enough pie for 4; a 9″ pie will serve 6 or more. Pastry
browns best on the bottom when baked in a glass pie

plate or dull-finish aluminum piepan. If you bake in a foil piepan, put it on a baking sheet so that bottom crust will brown evenly.

Freezing Pies

• Pie shells can be frozen baked or unbaked. Frozen baked shells will keep 4 months; unbaked shells, 2 months. To thaw baked shells, unwrap and let stand at room temperature. Or put in 350°F. oven about 6 minutes. Unbaked shells can be baked in the frozen state.

• Fruit pies are best if baked before freezing.

• Do not freeze custard, cream or meringue pies. Custard and cream fillings separate; meringues toughen and shrink.

• Freeze pies first, then wrap and store. Use heavyweight plastic wrap and seal with freezer tape, heavyduty foil, sealed with a tight double fold, plastic bags or other airtight containers. Label and date. Pies will keep 4 to 6 months. Store chiffon pies only 1 month.

• To heat baked pies, unwrap and let stand 30 minutes; heat in 350°F. oven just until warm.

• To thaw chiffon pies, unwrap and let stand at room temperature 2 to 4 hours. Chiffon pies may be eaten while still partially frozen.

BUTTERSCOTCH CREAM PIE

½ cup granulated sugar
2 cups milk
¼ cup butter
½ cup all-purpose flour
¾ cup packed brown sugar

½ teaspoon salt
2 eggs
Baked 9″ pie shell
1 cup heavy cream, whipped
Toasted slivered almonds

Put granulated sugar in small heavy saucepan or skillet and cook without stirring until sugar melts and becomes golden brown. Remove from heat and add ⅓ cup hot water slowly; cook without stirring until sugar dissolves. Add milk and heat almost to boiling. Melt butter in top part of double boiler. Remove from heat and add mixture of flour, brown sugar and salt; beat in eggs. Slowly add caramel-milk mixture. Cook over boiling water until thickened, stirring constantly; cover and cook 10 minutes, stirring occasionally. Cool to room temperature. Pour into baked shell. Chill several hours. Spread with whipped cream; sprinkle with nuts.

PRALINE APPLE PIE

2½ cups sliced peeled
   apples
⅓ cup granulated sugar
¼ teaspoon each nutmeg
   and cinnamon
Unbaked 9″ pie shell

2 tablespoons honey
½ cup packed brown sugar
2 tablespoons butter or
   margarine
1 egg, beaten
½ cup pecans

Combine apples, granulated sugar and spices. Put in pie shell. Bake in hot oven (400°F.) 15 minutes. Mix next 3 ingredients; bring to a boil. Add egg and nuts. Remove pie from oven and pour honey mixture over top. Return to 400°F. oven 10 minutes. Then reduce heat to 325°F. and bake 25 to 30 minutes longer, or until pie is set and apples are soft. Serve warm.

EARLY AMERICAN FRESH PEAR PIE

Especially delicious served warm.

¾ cup sugar
2 tablespoons flour
½ teaspoon each nutmeg
  and cinnamon

6 cups thinly sliced peeled
  ripe pears
Pastry for 2-crust 9" pie
2 tablespoons butter

Mix first 3 ingredients; add pears and mix lightly. Line piepan with half of pastry. Add filling and dot with butter. Adjust top crust. Bake in hot oven (425°F.) about 50 minutes. Serve warm or cold.

CHESS PIE

Raisins, dates and walnuts in a brown-sugar-and-cream mixture.

2 eggs
1½ tablespoons all-purpose
  flour
⅔ cup packed brown sugar
½ teaspoon salt
1 teaspoon vanilla extract

1 cup heavy cream
½ cup seedless raisins
1 cup cut-up pitted dates
1 cup broken walnut meats
Unbaked 9" pie shell

Beat the eggs until thick and lemon-colored. Mix the next 3 ingredients. Add to eggs and beat well. Stir in remaining ingredients, except pie shell. Spoon into shell. Bake in moderate oven (350°F.) 50 minutes, or until a silver knife inserted in center comes out clean. Cool.

FROZEN LEMON PIE

4 eggs, separated
Grated rind of 1 lemon
⅓ cup lemon juice
⅔ cup sugar

1 cup heavy cream, whipped
⅛ teaspoon salt
⅓ cup fine graham-cracker
   crumbs

In the top part of double boiler mix egg yolks, the lemon rind and juice and sugar. Cook over hot water until thickened, stirring. Cool. Fold in cream and egg whites, beaten stiff with salt. Butter a 9" piepan and sprinkle with half the crumbs. Pour in lemon mixture and sprinkle with remaining crumbs. Freeze until firm.

KEY LIME PIE

¼ cup lime juice
1 envelope unflavored
   gelatin
1 cup sugar
¼ teaspoon salt

4 eggs, separated
Freshly grated lime rind
Baked 8" pastry shell or
   crumb crust
Sweetened whipped cream

In the top part of small double boiler, put the lime juice and ½ cup water. Soften gelatin in liquids. Add ½ cup sugar, the salt and egg yolks. Beat slightly to blend. Cook over simmering water, stirring constantly until mixture is thickened and coats a metal spoon. Remove from heat and add 2 teaspoons rind. Chill until thickened but not firm. Beat egg whites until foamy; gradually add remaining ½ cup sugar, beating until stiff. Fold into gelatin. Pile lightly in shell; chill until firm. Spread with cream; sprinkle with lime rind.

BLUEBERRY PIE WITH CREAM-CHEESE TOPPING

Wash and drain 1 quart fresh blueberries. Put in saucepan with grated rind and juice of 1 lemon. Cover and cook 5 minutes. Mix ¾ cup sugar, 3 tablespoons cornstarch and ¼ teaspoon salt. Stir into berries and cook, stirring, until thickened. Cool and pour into baked 9″ pie shell. Beat 3 ounces cream cheese with 2 tablespoons cream; decorate cold pie.

DEEP-DISH PEACH PIE

¼ cup sugar	4 cups sliced peeled
½ cup packed light-brown	firm-ripe peaches
sugar	2 tablespoons lemon juice
⅛ teaspoon mace	Pastry for 1-crust pie,
1½ tablespoons quick-	unbaked
cooking tapioca	Cream

Combine first 4 ingredients. Add peaches and lemon juice and toss gently to mix. Turn into 9″ square baking dish. Roll pastry to about an 11″ square. Put over peaches, pressing to side of dish. Cut a few slits in top with knife to permit steam to escape. Bake in hot oven (425°F.) 40 minutes, or until crust is browned and filling is bubbly. Serve with cream while still warm.

MINCEMEAT PIE WITH CHEESE CRUST

1½ cups all-purpose sifted
flour
½ teaspoon salt
⅓ cup shortening

½ cup shredded process
American cheese
4 cups prepared mincemeat
¼ cup brandy (optional)

Sift flour and salt; then cut in shortening. Add the cheese and toss with fork to blend. Sprinkle with cold water (about 2 tablespoons). Mix with fork until dry ingredients are moistened. Press into a ball. On floured board, roll ⅔ of dough to ⅛" thickness; press into 9" piepan. Fill with mincemeat, mixed with the brandy, if used. Roll remaining dough and cut in strips ½" wide. Arrange on pie, lattice fashion. Trim lattice edges and crimp edges of crust with fingers. Bake in hot oven (400°F.) 20 minutes, or until lightly browned.

BLACK BOTTOM PIE

4 teaspoons cornstarch
⅛ teaspoon salt
1 cup sugar
4 eggs, separated
2 cups milk, scalded
1 package (6 ounces) semisweet chocolate pieces

2 teaspoons vanilla extract
Baked 9" pie shell
1 envelope unflavored
gelatin
¼ teaspoon cream of tartar

In top part of double boiler, mix cornstarch, salt and ½ cup sugar. Beat egg yolks and stir in milk. Add to first mixture and cook, stirring, over simmering water until mixture thickens and coats a spoon. Remove from

heat, measure 1 cup and pour over ½ cup chocolate
pieces. Beat with fork until smooth. Add 1 teaspoon
vanilla, cool and pour into shell. Chill. Soften gelatin in
¼ cup cold water, add remaining hot mixture and stir
until gelatin is dissolved. Add 1 teaspoon vanilla and
chill until thickened. Beat egg whites until foamy; add
cream of tartar and beat until almost stiff. Gradually
add remaining ½ cup sugar and continue beating until
stiff. Fold into gelatin mixture and pour over chocolate layer. Sprinkle with remaining ½ cup chocolate,
chopped. Chill until firm.

DEVONSHIRE STRAWBERRY TARTS

*Cream cheese is covered with whole berries and a
strained-berry filling.*

1 quart strawberries	1 package (3 ounces) cream
¼ cup cornstarch	cheese
Dash of salt	2 tablespoons milk
¾ cup sugar	6 baked shallow 4″ tart
	shells

Wash and hull berries; put half through sieve. Add
enough water to sieved berries to make 1½ cups. Mix
cornstarch, the salt and sugar; stir in sieved berries.
Cook 5 minutes, or until thick, stirring constantly. Cool.
Mix cheese with milk; spread in bottom of tart shells;
cover with whole berries, tips up; top with cornstarch
mixture. Chill. Makes 6 servings.

NUT PASTRIES

1 cup soft butter or
   margarine
3 cups all-purpose flour
1 package active dry yeast
3 egg yolks

1 cup dairy sour cream
1 teaspoon vanilla extract
Nut Filling
Confectioners' sugar

Cut butter into flour. Soften yeast in 2 tablespoons warm water. Add to flour mixture with remaining ingredients, except filling and sugar. Mix thoroughly and chill a few hours. Roll dough to 1/8" thickness on floured board. Cut in 3" squares. Put 1 teaspoon filling in center of each square. Moisten edges of pastry with water and pinch corners up and together. Bake on ungreased cookie sheets in moderate oven (375°F.) about 15 minutes. Cool and sprinkle with sugar. Makes about 4 dozen.

Nut Filling Force 4 cups walnuts through food chopper, using medium blade. Add 1 cup sugar, 3 tablespoons vanilla and 1/2 cup milk; mix well.

SOUTH AMERICAN COCONUT PASTRIES

2 cups all-purpose flour
1/2 teaspoon baking powder
1/2 teaspoon salt
1/2 cup butter

5 tablespoons orange juice
1 egg white
Coconut Filling

Sift dry ingredients into bowl; cut in butter. Mix in orange juice, a little at a time, until ball of dough is formed. (Dough will be rather dry.) Press together lightly. Wrap in waxed paper and chill 1 hour. Roll the dough ⅛″ thick on a lightly floured board. Cut with a 3½″ cookie cutter. Put 1 teaspoon Coconut Filling on half of each round. Moisten edges and fold over. Seal edges with a fork. Arrange on greased baking sheet and brush with slightly beaten egg white. Bake in hot oven (425°F.) 10 minutes, or until delicately browned. Makes 1½ to 2 dozen.

Coconut Filling Mix 1½ cups flaked coconut, 1 tablespoon cornstarch, ⅓ cup sugar and ¾ cup undiluted evaporated milk. Cook over low heat, stirring 5 minutes. Add 2 beaten egg yolks and 3 tablespoons melted butter, stirring. Stir over low heat 2 minutes. Cool.

PRESERVES, PICKLES, RELISHES

SHOPPING FOR PICKLES &
PRESERVES INGREDIENTS

Every market offers a selection of excellent commercial pickles, preserves, jams, jellies and relishes. But when you're in the mood for something different, something more distinctive, consider one of the recipes in this chapter.

For preserving, select firm fruit and vegetables, free from blemishes and spots. If ripe fruit is called for, be sure it is thoroughly ripe but not overripe or jellies won't set. Wash all foods just before you use them.

For pickling, use a good clear standard vinegar, free from sediment, one with 4 to 6 percent acidity; strength of vinegar is usually shown on the bottle label. If vinegar or brine is too weak, the pickles will spoil or become soft. Distilled white vinegar is best for preserving the color and crispness of foods.

Use a pure granulated salt for pickling. Granulated salt containing less than 1 percent chemicals is satisfactory.

Use soft water if possible. Large amounts of calcium and other salts found in many hard waters may interfere with the fermentation and pickling processes. High iron content in water may cause food to darken. If hard water must be used, boil, skim off scum and let water stand 24 hours. Ladle water off the top, leaving the sediment in the bottom.

White corn syrup or honey can replace half the sugar called for. Use 1 cup for each cup of sugar replaced. Stir frequently during cooking.

Pickling Equipment

Select jars of glasses without nicks or cracks. Wash jars and lids thoroughly. Sterilize jars for pickles by boiling in water to cover 15 minutes; treat lids and rubbers, if used, according to manufacturer's directions. Let stand in water until needed. Jars and glasses used for jellies, jams and spreads need not be sterilized, just brought to a boil. Use a wooden spoon and a large shallow kettle for cooking. Fill jars with hot pickles and preserves to within ¼″ of top. Always follow the manufacturer's directions for sealing the jars. Use crockery, glass, earthenware or stainless steel for brining, but not aluminum or any chipped enamelware. If cucumbers, peppers and onions are to stand overnight in salt solution, put in refrigerator to prevent fermenting.

STORAGE

When cold, label jars with name and date and store in cool, dark, dry place. Jellies and jams may need a little time to set, and most develop best flavor after standing a few weeks.

BEST-EVER PICKLED ONION RINGS

Large sweet onions
2 cups white vinegar
1 cup sugar
1 teaspoon each mustard
  seed, celery seed and

ground turmeric
¼ teaspoon powdered alum
  (buy in drugstore)

Peel and slice ⅛" thick enough onions to fill a wide-mouthed quart jar. Bring remaining ingredients to boil and pour over onions. Cool, then cover and refrigerate. Let stand several days before serving. Will keep several months.

ZUCCHINI PICKLES

Build an antipasto plate around these with tuna, olives, chick-peas, artichokes and hard-cooked eggs.

2 pounds small zucchini
2 medium onions
¼ cup salt
1 pint white vinegar
1 cup sugar

1 teaspoon celery seed
1 teaspoon turmeric
½ teaspoon dry mustard
1 teaspoon mustard seed

Wash and cut unpeeled zucchini and peeled onions in very thin slices into crock or bowl. Cover with water and add salt. Let stand 1 hour; drain. Mix remaining ingredients and bring up to boil. Pour over zucchini and onion. Let stand 1 hour. Bring to boil and cook 3 minutes. Pack in 3 hot sterilized pint jars and seal.

APRICOT-HORSERADISH RELISH

To serve with sliced cold meats.

⅓ cup cider vinegar
½ cup sugar
⅔ cup bottled horseradish, undrained
6 whole cloves
1 cup seedless raisins
1 cup chopped dried apricots
⅓ cup sliced, blanched almonds

Combine vinegar, 1 cup water, sugar, horseradish and cloves. Boil 5 minutes. Add fruits and nuts; simmer 15 minutes more. Cover and refrigerate. Makes about 2 cups.

TOMATO-FRUIT RELISH

30 large ripe tomatoes (about 12 pounds)
6 medium peaches
6 medium pears
2 large onions
3 cups sugar
1½ cups chopped celery
3 tablespoons salt
1 quart white vinegar
2 tablespoons mixed pickling spice

Peel first 4 ingredients and chop fine. Add next 4 ingredients, and pickling spice tied in a piece of cheesecloth. Boil, uncovered, 1 to 1½ hours. Remove spice bag. Pour into hot sterilized jars and seal. Makes about 5 pints.

PEACH CHUTNEY

A spicy condiment of fruit seasoned with garlic, ginger and vinegar.

3½ cups sugar
2 cups white vinegar
1 quart chopped peeled
 firm peaches
1½ cups raisins or dried
 currants

1 clove garlic, minced
4 pieces whole dried ginger
 or 3 pieces preserved
 ginger, chopped

Heat sugar and vinegar to boiling in large kettle. Add peaches, raisins and garlic. Add whole ginger, tied in cheesecloth bag, or add chopped ginger. Bring to boil and cook slowly, uncovered, 2 hours, or until thick, stirring occasionally. Remove whole ginger. Ladle into 4 hot sterilized half-pint jars and seal.

PLUM CONSERVE

Tossing orange rind with sugar to draw out flavor makes this unusually good.

3 pounds (about 1¾ quarts)
 blue plums or fresh prunes
3 medium oranges
1½ cups seeded raisins,
 chopped

1¼ cups seedless raisins
6 cups sugar
½ cup chopped nuts

Remove pits from plums. Peel oranges, reserving rinds, and dice pulp. Combine raisins, plums and orange pulp. Add 5½ cups sugar and mix well. Let stand overnight in refrigerator. Cook orange rind in boiling water until tender. Cut off and discard white inner lining. Dice remaining rind and sprinkle with ½ cup sugar. Let stand overnight in refrigerator. Combine both mixtures in kettle, bring to boil and cook, stirring frequently, 30 minutes, or until thickened. Add nuts 5 minutes before removing from heat. Turn into 7 hot sterilized 6-ounce glasses. Cover with melted paraffin.

PEACH-ORANGE MARMALADE

18 medium peaches   10 cups sugar
6 oranges

Scald, peel and dice peaches. Squeeze the juice from oranges and grind skins, using medium blade. Combine ingredients, cover and let stand overnight. Cook over low heat, stirring until sugar is dissolved. Bring to boil and cook over moderate heat 1 hour, stirring frequently to prevent scorching, until clear and thickened. Pour into hot sterilized jars and seal at once. Makes about 3½ quarts.

JUNE JAM

Fresh rhubarb and pineapple are combined with strawberries.

3 cups shredded fresh
  pineapple
2 cups cut fresh rhubarb

4 cups hulled washed
  strawberries
Dash of salt
4½ cups sugar

Put pineapple in large preserving kettle and cook without added liquid 10 minutes. Add rhubarb, berries and salt; cook 20 minutes. Add sugar, bring to boil and boil rapidly, stirring frequently, 25 to 30 minutes, or until thick. Skim off foam and pour into hot sterilized jars. Seal wtih hot paraffin, cover with lids and store in a cool place. Makes about 6 half-pint jars.

INDEX

A

B

We hope you enjoy the many delicious, nutritious recipes in the **Woman's Day Collector's Cookbook.** Take it into your kitchen with the confidence that you take Fuller Brush fine quality homecare and personal care products into your home. Each product proudly displays the Fuller Brush name . . . from kitchen cleaners, to carpet and floor care, to laundry aids and clothing organizers, to the creams, lotions and personal brushes that help you to more beautiful skin and hair.

Ask your Fuller Brush Representative for a demonstration of Fuller Brush products. For 77 years, millions of Americans have been enjoying fine quality Fuller products and the personalized service of their Fuller Representative!

The Fuller Brush Company and Your Independent
Fuller Brush Representative

THE FULLER BRUSH COMPANY • GREAT BEND, KANSAS 67530
ℰ A Consolidated Foods Company • Responsive To Consumer Needs